your child's
dog

your
child's
dog

Andrea McHugh

How to help
your kids care
for their pets

Published by Firefly Books Ltd. 2007

Copyright © 2007 Octopus Publishing Group Ltd.

First printing

Publisher Cataloging-in-Publication Data (U.S.)

McHugh, Andrea.
   Your child's dog : how to help your kids care for their pets / Andrea McHugh.
[128] p. : col. photos. ;   cm.
Includes index.
Summary: A dog-care manual that shows parents and guardians how to involve children in every aspect of looking after their dogs. Chapters cover: deciding to get a dog; choosing a dog; preparing the family and the house for the dog; settling in a new dog; setting up a day-to-day routine, including socialization and habituation, feeding, grooming, bathing, health checks, play and exercise, and dog behavior, training, health and safety.
ISBN-13: 978-1-55407-304-7 (pbk.)
ISBN-10: 1-55407-304-9 (pbk.)
   1. Dogs. 2. children and animals. I. Title.
636.7/0887 dc22   SF426.M347   2007

Library and Archives Canada Cataloguing in Publication

McHugh, Andrea
   Your child's dog : how to help your kids care for th / Andrea McHugh.
Includes index.
ISBN-13: 978-1-55407-304-7
ISBN-10: 1-55407-304-9
   1. Dogs. 2. Children and animals. I. Title.
SF426.5.M32 2007   636.7'0887   C2007-902611-7

Published in the United States by
Firefly Books (U.S.) Inc.
P.O. Box 1338, Ellicott Station
Buffalo, New York 14205

Published in Canada by
Firefly Books Ltd.
66 Leek Crescent
Richmond Hill, Ontario L4B 1H1

Printed in China

Notes

The advice given here should not be used as a substitute for that of a veterinary surgeon. No dogs or puppies were harmed in the making of this book.

Unless the information given in this book is specifically for female dogs, dogs are referred to throughout as 'he'. Unless otherwise specified, the information is applicable equally to male and female dogs.

Contents

Introduction

There is no doubt that a dog can bring a huge amount of pleasure and fun to the whole family. Having a pet like a dog will also help your child learn important lessons about being responsible for the health and well-being of another living creature. However, looking after a dog properly requires time, commitment and effort, and it will change the way your family lives. This is something that is not always easy to convey to children. If you are a parent or guardian and you find yourself being put under pressure to buy a dog, then this is the book for you.

Your Child's Dog has been written to give you, the responsible adult, an understanding of exactly what is involved in caring for a dog, and the words to explain things in ways that children will understand. Simply telling a child not to carry a puppy everywhere like a toy will probably go in one ear and out the other. After all, a cute puppy looks just like a toy, and a determined child will just find its wriggling endearing. However, if you can explain the reasons why a dog doesn't like to be carried (because it feels insecure and vulnerable without the use of its legs to run away from danger), you will help even a young child to imagine how the puppy is feeling.

Using simple step-by-step instructions, *Your Child's Dog* also shows how children can be involved in every aspect of looking after their pet, so that you don't need to worry that you will be left with all the chores as soon as the novelty wears off. As well as demonstrating how to get your child stuck into the routine care, such as feeding, exercising and grooming, there's also lots of information about teaching children to train a puppy from scratch. Helping your child train a dog to sit, walk on a leash and roll over will strengthen the bond between child and puppy — and also take much of the responsibility for training out of your hands.

You'll also discover how to involve your child in the less exciting aspects of dog ownership, such as checking for fleas, bathing and visiting the vet. Each stage of a dog's life has its own challenges, and your child will need help to learn how to

deal with these and to behave in a way that will ensure that the puppy remains happy and well as it becomes an adult.

As a first step, you need to decide as a family whether you are able to offer a home to a dog or whether it would be better to defer the decision for a while. When you are certain that you are ready and able to become a dog-owning family, the next stage is to do your research and decide on the best type of dog for you. And once you've chosen your puppy, you need to prepare your home and your children for the new arrival. This includes discussing how responsibility will be allocated among different members of the family and making sure the house and yard are puppy-friendly zones.

Once you have brought the dog home, you are faced with a whole new set of questions and potential problems. How can your child and dog play safely together? How do you deal with bad behavior from puppy or child? And how do you answer all those awkward or embarrassing questions? Look out for the "Question time" boxes, which pose all the questions that children commonly ask. In each case, you'll find an explanation of the underlying issues as well as a sample answer couched in terms that your child should find easy to understand.

Learning as much as possible about canine behavior, and about the way that dogs communicate with each other and with their owners, means that you and your family will get maximum enjoyment from your dog. And, after all, having fun together is what owning a dog is all about.

chapter 1

Can we get a dog?

This chapter is all about deciding whether you are ready and able to welcome a puppy into your family. "Please, can I have a dog?" is probably a request that you've heard quite often. Most children would love to own a puppy, dreaming of cuddling it every night and having fun together. Unfortunately, they don't usually think much beyond that, and their knowledge tends to be gleaned from fictional characters, like Scooby Doo and Snoopy. These cartoon dogs are heroic, talking animals, that are more than capable of looking after themselves and their owners. The reality, of course, is that a dog needs a lot of care and attention.

Under pressure

Children decide that they want a dog for all sorts of reasons, which range from peer pressure to a new film or book that's just come out featuring a doggy hero. They can exert significant pressure on their parents, and busy working people often give in through guilt or the desire for a quiet life. Unfortunately, dogs that are acquired in these circumstances often have to be rehomed when the novelty wears off and the children's initial enthusiasm fades.

It's no use telling your children, "You'll have to walk the dog every day and feed it and groom it." A desperate child will automatically say, "I will! I promise! Please, please! I'll look after it for the rest of my life and love you forever." Does this sound familiar? There are wonderful advantages for the whole family in owning a dog, and some of these are described later in the book (see pages 12–13, for example), but it's still important to do your homework thoroughly before you buy one. When you know exactly what is involved, you can decide as a family whether you are in a position to bring a dog into your lives and provide it with a good home.

Fast forward

Before you agree that your child can have a puppy and start to bask in the glow of gratitude and their assurances that you are the best parent in the world, take a few moments to think about the time when that appealing puppy is a large, boisterous hound. Imagine a wet, dark, wintry morning. Your child has some homework to finish and, in any case, you are not thrilled that she go outdoors in the dark, even with a dog. So, it's up to you to put on your coat and venture outdoors. The problem is that nobody has trained the dog, who won't come back when it's called. You miss breakfast and are late for work. As if that's not bad enough, when you get home you find that the dog has destroyed your favorite cushion and chewed the leg of a chair. You stare open-mouthed — Scooby Doo and Snoopy never behaved like that.

Thankfully, careful planning and the commitment of the whole family will enable you to avoid days like that. Learning to share with your child the care of your dog and responsibility for it will allow you all to enjoy the loving companionship of a loyal and well-behaved family friend.

What a dog owner
provides

Considering what a dog requires to be happy and healthy is the first step to deciding whether you can provide a good home for one. You should also think about your own lifestyle and how it might be affected by having a dog. Like a new baby, a puppy turns family life upside down, and your responsibility for the animal will continue for many years after it has been trained.

Your circumstances

As an initial step, think about where you live, how many children you have (or are planning to have), your child's personality and the time you all will have available to spend with the dog. Remember to factor in any time spent on other activities, such as baseball, ballet lessons or music practice, which may have to be given up. You should also calculate how much of the household budget you can comfortably afford for a dog's care, including regular visits to the vet.

When your child first asks if he can have a puppy, it is worth sitting down together and making a checklist of a dog's basic requirements. It is important to explain to your child that a dog needs to be given everything on this list if it is to be happy and healthy — and not just the fun-sounding aspects like play and cuddling. Most children will find that words like "training" and "socialization" sound exceptionally dull, but do point out to them that these aspects of a dog's care can actually turn out to be the most fun and most rewarding.

Can you supply these?

Fresh water
Good-quality dog food
Shelter from the elements
Exercise and play
Grooming
Freedom from pain
Routine veterinary care
Socialization (getting your dog used to strange noises and people)
Training
Mental stimulation
Affection and companionship

How much time?

The main thing a dog needs from you and your child is time. Puppies vary enormously in how long it takes them to become house-broken and settled into a new home, but this is a stage that you must all be prepared to work on. Training basic obedience and, most importantly, teaching your child how to handle and work with the dog will also take time and patience, and you also need to think about the time you will spend on general care, including walking, playing, feeding and grooming.

Spontaneous sleepovers at friends' houses will become a thing of the past, because you will always have to consider the dog and make arrangements for its care. This can be a shock to a family that has never owned a pet before, and it is important to consider whether everyone is willing to accept these constraints.

How much money?

Dogs can be expensive, particularly if they become sick and need veterinary treatment, and budgeting for an annual or monthly pet insurance policy is important. If you are planning to buy a purebred, expect to pay much more than you would for a crossbreed or mongrel.

Other costs

Boarding fees if you go away on vacation
Dog food
Essential items, such as a bed, collar, leash and identity tag and food and water bowls
Microchipping
A pet passport if you intend to travel with your dog
Dog training classes

How long?

Barring illness and accidents, large and giant breeds, such as Great Danes and German Shepherds, live for eight to 10 years, while smaller breeds, such as Jack Russell Terriers and Yorkshire Terriers, can live into their late teens. Your child may well be leaving home to go to college when the dog is still in its prime and you could become the sole carer at a time when you may well be looking forward to freedom from responsibilities. On the positive side, having a dog can help to fill the gap when a child leaves the nest, and the routine of caring for it can relieve stress and provide companionship.

ABOVE LEFT: Regular grooming is essential to keep your dog's coat clean and tangle-free.

ABOVE RIGHT: Border Collies were originally bred to herd sheep and need lots of exercise and stimulation.

OPPOSITE: Leading the puppy outside to relieve itself after feeding is one easy way in which your child can take responsibility for its care.

Tip to parents

To help you prepare a budget, visit your vet and find out how much the dog's vaccinations, flea treatments, heartworm prevention and check-ups are likely to cost, then allow extra for emergencies.

Right reasons
for getting a puppy

Parents should never feel obliged to get a dog to mend a guilty conscience because they are too busy to spend time with their children. Ultimately, they won't have time for the dog, either. Similarly, buying a dog to cheer up a child after the parents separate or divorce will help only if the parent with whom the child lives has sufficient time and money for the extra commitment.

Benefits

As well as providing an immense amount of fun, owning a dog and taking responsibility for it offers a child valuable life lessons, including developing empathy and concern for the welfare of others, and dealing with loss. Research has shown that there are also many other benefits from owning a pet. For example, studies have found that:

Children with pets tend to be fitter and more sociable than those without.
Autistic children with pets show more pro-social behaviors and less autistic behaviors than those without pets.
Teenage pet owners living in deprived areas are more content and have better relationships with adults than their peers without pets.
Children exposed to pets during the first year of life have a lower frequency of allergic rhinitis (hayfever) and asthma.

Disadvantages

When you are considering getting a dog, remember that there are several disadvantages, the most serious of which is probably lack of freedom. You must always arrange for the dog's care when you go away or are likely to be delayed, and, if you already lead a very busy life,

LEFT: Choose a quiet time of year to bring your puppy home (avoid Christmas or birthdays), so that it can settle in with minimum fuss.

OPPOSITE ABOVE: If you have a baby, it may be a good idea to choose a small breed known to be gentle. Dogs should never be left unsupervised with small children.

with lots of other commitments, it might be better to wait to get a dog until the whole family has more time.

Don't forget that a dog will add to the family budget. Vet's bills, food, insurance and boarding fees when you are away on vacation can be significant items, so think carefully before taking on the extra burden.

Some people are afraid of or allergic to animals. Think about how you would cope with this if you introduced a dog into your home. Also, if you are very particular about the appearance of your home you should think about how you will deal with the inevitable mess that having a dog will bring.

Baby love

Some children are born into households where there is already a family pet, and, if steps are taken to make sure that the dog doesn't become jealous or isolated, there is no reason why significant problems should arise. However, buying a puppy when you have a new baby is probably not a good idea, even if you think it would be "nice for them grow up together." Juggling the very demanding care of a new puppy and a baby may well mean that someone will miss out.

If you would like to have a dog but are uncertain whether your children have reached an appropriate age, consider how much responsibility you expect them to assume for the dog's well-being (see pages 14–15).

Question time

Q *Can I have a puppy for my birthday?*
Much as this may be your child's dream present, it is better to wait until after the actual day. Explain this to your child, but give a gift-wrapped dog collar, leash or bowl as reassurance that the dream will come true.

A The puppy won't be very happy to arrive on your birthday. There would be too much going on and it would be scared. All the visitors, loud noises and party games would mean it wouldn't get enough rest. Let's make a list of things we need for the puppy and ask people to get those for your birthday. We can get the dog later.

Q *When can I have a dog then?*
Patience is not usually a strong point with children. The beginning of the new school year will give the dog time to settle in while the children are at school.

A The best time is probably after the summer break, because we'll all have lots of time for the puppy then. You can enjoy playing with the dog before and after school, and it can rest while you are in class.

Who will care for the puppy?

Before you commit to getting a dog, decide who is going to be responsible for the different aspects of his care. Your discussion should cover responsibilities such as feeding, exercising and grooming, as well as cleaning up after the puppy. Encourage the children to draw up a schedule themselves, so that everyone knows exactly who would do what job and when.

ABOVE LEFT: Even very small children can take responsibility for keeping the puppy's water bowl topped up.

ABOVE RIGHT: Giving the puppy lots of affection is one duty that your children won't want to shirk!

OPPOSITE: Older children will enjoy feeding the dog, under adult supervision.

Sharing the load

There will be plenty of volunteers for the fun stuff, like playing with the puppy, but children may not be so keen to help when it comes to tidying up or doing the "dirty" jobs, like grooming. Allocating particular tasks to everyone in the family provides an opportunity for them to bond with the dog and will help the puppy become a real member of the family.

Take into account your children's ages and their physical and mental abilities and always supervise them. Even toddlers can be allocated simple tasks, such as fetching the dog's food from the pantry when it's feeding time, and putting it away again afterward. Older children can accompany an adult on walks, participate in training, go to puppy classes, learn how to groom the dog and help with many other tasks.

Inevitably there will be some mess involved in keeping a dog. You can expect muddy paws on the kitchen floor and fur on the carpet, so decide who will help clean up. If it is always the same person who does this, it may cause resentment. Agreeing to take responsibility in turns, perhaps on a daily or weekly basis, will help to avoid turning cleaning into an issue.

Question time

Q *If I've got homework and football practice, will I still have to walk the dog?*
Encouraging children to help care for their dog every day, no matter what the weather or other activities, helps them to develop a sense of responsibility. If necessary, visit your vet's office and ask a member of the staff to explain the importance of a specific task, such as grooming, and how failure to do this properly will affect the dog's well-being.

A The dog will still need walking but perhaps we could do two jobs at once, such as walking to football practice and taking the dog with us or walking the dog to school and back each day. If you don't want to be involved in caring for the dog maybe we should get one later, when you are less busy.

There are lots of ways in which children can be involved in looking after the dog:

Getting dog food out at meal times and putting it away again; older children can feed the dog under supervision before and after school.

Washing, drying and putting away the dog's food and water dishes.

Checking and refilling the water bowls.

Fetching the dog's grooming kit and putting it away; older children can learn how to groom the dog.

Hanging up its collar and leash tidily.

Helping to do a weekly health check of paws, teeth, eyes and fur.

Keeping the dog's toy box tidy and clearing away their own toys so that the dog knows which toys are ok to play with, and which are not.

Spending some time playing with the dog each day.

Helping to walk the dog and washing and drying muddy paws afterward.

Learning how to mop a muddy floor and vacuum up dog hair from the carpets and the furniture.

Doing your
puppy
research

There is a lot you can do as a family to prepare for owning a dog. Start by doing as much research as possible into the different dog breeds, in order to find out which would be the best type for your family. Take into account where you live, how much space you have and how much free time everyone will have to spend on the dog.

Sources of information

The Internet is a great resource, with numerous breed sites available that allow you to see what the dogs will look like as puppies and adults and find out whether they are low- or high-maintenance. Your library will also stock a range of books on different breeds.

Make a note of the breeds that interest you and visit some dog shows to see them in action. Most people are only too happy to talk about their dogs, and as long as they are not waiting to go into a competition or are busy getting their dogs ready to show, you should be able to find out useful information, such as how good they are as family pets, how easy they are to look after and whether they require lots of exercise.

Helping hands

If your neighbor has a dog, ask if your children can help walk it occasionally. This is a good way of finding out if they will be as committed to walking a dog on a cold, wet morning as they are on a sunny afternoon. Ask your neighbor to explain what is involved and make sure that all the negative aspects are discussed, as well as the positive ones.

Many canine rescue centers and shelters rely on volunteers to help care for their dogs. Your family may enjoy becoming involved for a couple

LEFT: If you have access to the Internet, you will be able to visit many different websites about dog breeds and dog ownership.

OPPOSITE: Dogs have to be walked in cold, wet weather, too. Ask your neighbors if your child can come along whenever they walk their dogs — whatever the weather.

of hours each weekend, and as a bonus the dogs will benefit from the extra socialization with children, making it easier for staff to rehome them. Being involved with rescue dogs can help your family decide what kind of dog they like best as well as getting first-hand experience of the work involved. Statistics show that more dogs are rehomed during the first year of ownership than at any other time, simply because the families concerned didn't realize what having a dog really involved.

Saving plan

You can help your children develop a sense of commitment by encouraging them to do extra jobs around the house and save their pocket money to buy something for the dog, such as a collar, or to add to a dog-buying fund.

Question time

Q *Why do I have to learn so much about dogs before we get a puppy?*

The more children know, the more interested they should become. If their enthusiasm wanes at this stage, you can assume that the desire to have a dog is a passing whim and decide not to pursue dog ownership any further at the moment. Some of the learning activities you could try include: picking up pamphlets from your vet's office; joining the junior branch of your national kennel club; visiting dog-training classes to see a variety of dog activities, such as flyball, agility and obedience training; talking to as many dog owners as possible, both adult and children; subscribing to a dog-care magazine; and making a list of local dog breeders and arranging visits.

A Learning about dogs is fun, and the more everyone in the family knows, the better we can look after the dog and the happier it will be.

chapter 2

Preparing for the puppy

You've thought hard about how a dog will change family life and you've started your research into the different types and breeds of dog. Now it's time to find the puppy! This chapter explains what to consider when buying your dog and it also explores how to prepare your family for the arrival of a new member. This includes creating a set of rules for both the family and the puppy, and explaining to your child about life from a dog's point-of-view. Even the most good-natured dog has its breaking point and your child will need to respect that.

Which dogs make good family pets?

Some breeds, such as the Border Collie, which was originally bred to herd sheep, require a lot of mental and physical stimulation to keep them occupied. Other breeds, such as the Golden Retriever, which responds well to training, are more placid and have a reputation for being excellent family pets. Toy dogs, such as the Chihuahua, look appealing but can be difficult to housebreak and may not enjoy the constant attention of children. Large breeds can be gentle giants, but because of their size may accidentally knock over small children.

While any breed has the potential to be a good family pet, when there are children involved you need to find a puppy that can cope happily with family life and who is safe with children. Consider whether the breed is suitable for your children's age, bearing in mind that a large or strong dog may be difficult for your child to handle. A small but temperamental breed may also not be the best choice for boisterous children. Think about why your child wants a dog — is he looking for companionship or entertainment, for example?

You also need to take your own needs into consideration. Avoid giant breeds if you can't afford the upkeep and do not go for long-haired breeds if fur on the carpet will drive you crazy. Be honest about the time you will have available to spend with your dog.

If you are buying a purebred dog (see pages 20–21), you can find out information about the dog's characteristics and behavior by researching the breed thoroughly and talking to breeders. Consider what the dog was originally bred to do — herding, retrieving, hunting and so on.

Adult or puppy?

Most children would love to have a cute puppy, and one of the benefits of this is that they will be involved in every stage of the dog's development and training. However, puppies are a lot of work for the first few weeks, so you must be prepared to commit extra time and patience.

Sometimes an adult dog becomes available that would make a perfect family pet. Perhaps a family you know are moving or their personal circumstances have changed and they are no longer able to care for the dog properly. If this dog ticks all the boxes on your wish list and has already proved to be a good family pet, your children may be thrilled to take it on. A word of caution though: it is stressful for any dog to go to a new home, so be prepared for a period of adjustment.

Where to buy
your new puppy

Once you have decided to get a dog, it can be tempting to buy the first one you see. However, before you make a final choice, there are some other points to consider. Do you want a purebred or a non-purebred dog? Both have their advantages and disadvantages. And where will you find your dog? Bear in mind that pet stores and puppy farms are not the best sources.

Purebred or not?

There are advantages to buying a purebred puppy. You will be able to meet the breeder and at least one of the dog's parents, so you will be able to predict the dog's appearance as an adult as well as behavior traits and potential health problems. The dog will be fully vaccinated and socialized. You will also receive pedigree certificates and a family tree, and your dog will be able to compete in pedigree dog shows. There is also a downside, however: purebred breeds can be expensive, they are not always immediately available and some are susceptible to health problems. Some purebred breeds may even be targeted by thieves.

The alternative is to buy a crossbreed, for which two different purebred parents were mated, or a randomly bred dog, which is usually

Q *Can we get a Scooby Doo?*
Never give in to a child's wish to have a dog because it looks like one in a cartoon. Puppies grow up, and the reality of ownership is different from what is shown on television.

A Scooby Doo looks as if he's very big, and we may not have enough room for him. Let's sit down together and find a real dog that's perfect for our family. You can still call him Scooby if you want to.

Q *Which puppy shall we get?*
For a family pet it may be best to avoid a puppy that is extremely extroverted or shy. Look for one that plays with other puppies, is interested in its surroundings and is confident enough to bond with children.

A When we see the puppies, sit quietly and see which ones come to you, and that will help us decide which is the bravest or the most shy.

ABOVE: A small breed, such as a Dachshund, can be less intimidating for small children than a larger size of dog.

OPPOSITE: Friendly, playful and kind, Golden Retrievers are a popular choice for families.

LEFT: Border Terriers are affectionate, good-tempered and always ready to play.

the result of an accidental mating. These are less expensive and often more hardy than purebred dogs and less likely to be stolen. Non-purebred dogs are also easy to obtain and visually unique. However, problems may arise if the dog's family history is unknown. There is no guarantee how it will look as an adult and it may be susceptible to health problems. It may also not be vaccinated.

Questions to ask the breeder

Before you buy a purebred puppy draw up a list of questions. You will have to answer some questions, too, because reputable breeders are extremely fussy about rehoming their dogs. Questions you should ask include:

When were the puppies born?
Where have they been kept? (In the home is preferable to outside in a kennel.)
Can we see both parents?
Were any pre-breeding tests done that show the puppies could develop disease?

What are their temperaments like?
Are they used to other people and pets?
Have they been handled much?
Are they high- or low-maintenance dogs?
Are they vaccinated and microchipped?
Are they insured?

Where to buy?

Your children may be drawn to pet stores but these are not the best places to get a puppy, because you cannot be certain about the dog's background. Some puppies are bred in poor conditions on puppy farms and may, as a consequence, suffer health problems later. Buying a dog from a registered, reputable breeder is a much better option. Humane societies are also always full of dogs in need of good homes. Be prepared to undergo a home assessment and answer questions about your lifestyle, to help the organization suggest the dogs that are best suited to your family. Avoid puppy farms and unscrupulous breeders, and never, ever buy on impulse.

A puppy's place
in the family hierarchy

Before your new puppy comes home it is a good idea to think about where it is going to fit into the existing family hierarchy. Discuss this with your children and ask them to think about how they should react to the newcomer. It is important that the puppy realizes from the start that it is not, and never will be, the top dog in its pack, which consists of members of your household.

Pampered pooches

Initially, the puppy is bound to be the center of attention in the household, but if this continues for too long it can become stressful for the animal. Stressed dogs can exhibit behavioral problems, which may manifest in different ways, depending on personality type. Housebreaking problems, constant barking, chewing or self-harm, such as obsessive overlicking of fur, can all be symptoms of stress. In addition, overpampered pooches do not make great family pets because they become demanding and disruptive.

Top dogs

The puppy must be taught that the adults in the house are at the top of the family hierarchy, with the children after that, followed by any existing pets and, finally, at the bottom of the pile, the new puppy. Dominant behavior that can be appealing in a little puppy will not be acceptable in a mature dog. If a dog is allowed to assume

Do!

Arrange for the puppy to be neutered or spayed as early as is recommended
Feed the puppy after other family members and other pets
Allocate a sleeping area for the puppy
Be consistent with rules
Enroll in a puppy training class

Don't! encourage your child to . . .

Feed treats indiscriminately
Play chasing or tug-of-war games

ABOVE: Holding a toy up high can be perceived by the dog as an invitation to jump up and grab it.

RIGHT: If your children say "no" to the puppy and stop playing with it as soon as it nips or chews, it will soon learn to behave.

OPPOSITE: If you don't want your dog on the sofa, make sure it knows that its place is always on the floor and don't let the children allow it to break the rules.

the role of top dog in the house, it will allocate itself the best chair, help itself to anything it wants to eat, including from your children's plates, take ownership of the children's toys, and become quite intimidating as it growls warnings at anyone who walks past. Many of these dogs are eventually labeled "bad dogs" and end up in a rehoming center, where, at best, they undergo a lengthy behavior therapy program before being rehomed. At worst, they will be euthanized.

The only way to avoid this difficult situation developing is to create a set of family house rules from day one and adhere to them. It is not necessary to resort to shouting or turn into some kind of autocratic monster. Simply being firm, fair and consistent about when and where the puppy is fed and where it is allowed to sit and sleep, and immediately stopping any games that encourage the dog to think it can be dominant over the children, is sufficient. For example, feed the family before the puppy gets its dinner, don't allow the puppy to walk through doorways in front of you or the children, and don't allow the dog to always win games.

Just say "no"

Teach your child how to say a firm "no" to the puppy if it does something unacceptable, such as nipping her fingers or chewing clothes. Explain that, for the puppy's own good, she should stop

playing with it immediately so that it realizes that any nipping or chewing will end the game and make life less fun. Drumming fingers on the floor to encourage a puppy to pounce on them will inevitably encourage it to try to gnaw at them. Ask your children to wave a toy for the puppy to catch and chew instead.

It's a
dog's
world

Encouraging your children to learn about canine behavior will help them to understand how dogs view the world. For instance, a dog can hear things that humans couldn't possibly pick up without special equipment. Often, when a dog appears to behave strangely, it can be a reaction to something it has heard and perceived to be dangerous, such as a distant thunderstorm.

Approaching a strike dog

1 The golden rule for approaching a strange dog is always to ask the owner first if you can stroke or pet it. The sweetest looking dogs can snap at a child, because of fear or a previous bad experience. Don't allow your child to approach a dog if the dog is overexcited or there are too many other children trying to pet it. Don't allow your child to approach a dog if she has food on her skin or clothing, for example if she's just been eating ice cream.

2 Observe the dog's body language. Does it look happy and confident or is it cowering behind its owner or looking hostile? If you are happy with the situation, and the owner gives permission, allow your child to approach the dog slowly. Remember that sudden actions can be perceived as frightening. During the approach, the child can hold out a hand slowly, palm down, and allow the dog to sniff.

No worries

Tell your children that, as much as possible, it's best to ignore a dog's fearful reactions if it is frightened by loud noises, even though it is tempting to pick the dog up and offer lots of cuddling. Unfortunately, if you do this you will confirm to the dog that there must be something for it to worry about and make it feel worse. See pages 118–19 for some tips on how you can help your dog to cope with nerves.

Good looking

Children should know that dogs tend to view staring by another dog as a confrontational act. Unfortunately, small children are often at a dog's eye-level height, and so it is important to train puppies from the beginning to accept eye contact with people. You can do this by regularly getting down to the puppy's level and spending time playing with it, talking to it, stroking its face and reassuring it so that it remains confident and finds this a positive, rewarding experience.

Safety first

Studies carried out in the United States reveal that dog bites are the second most common medical emergency, and smaller children are the most likely victims. If you have done your research thoroughly and chosen a breed with a reputation as a good family pet you will significantly decrease the risk of biting injury. However, any dog will bite if it is sufficiently provoked. Always supervise young children when they are around dogs and never leave them alone together. Discourage children from grabbing dogs around the neck and teach them how to approach a strange dog.

3 If the dog seems receptive and wants to come closer, encourage your child to stroke the dog gently on the back of its head.

Question time

Q *Why do dogs wag their tails and growl at the same time?*
Because they are confused. Something — perhaps meeting a new dog — has aroused their suspicion, and they don't know whether to play or fight.

A Tail wagging can be a little like waving a white flag in a dangerous situation, and the growling is a verbal warning.

Q *Why do dogs lick each other? And why do they lick us? It tickles!*
Dogs lick each other in greeting. Young dogs tend to lick as a sign of submissiveness to older dogs. It is up to you whether you tolerate licking of humans, but it is not very hygienic.

A It's how a dog says hello. Its mother licked it when it was born, to let it know her smell. It's not a good idea to let a dog lick you, as it could spread germs, and it should never lick your face. Say "no" and give the dog a toy to lick instead. Always wash your hands if a dog licks you.

A puppy's needs
in his new home

Before you bring your puppy home, you will have to consider how you will supply all its physical needs. Every puppy requires good-quality dog food, fresh water, routine, exercise, companionship, shelter from the elements and a safe space to call its own. It is also a good idea to register with a vet before the puppy arrives and arrange an appointment for its first checkup.

Food

Puppies normally go to their new homes when they have been vaccinated, which is usually between seven and 10 weeks old. This can be a stressful time for them, and any sudden dietary changes can result in gastric problems. To make the transition period easier, stock up on food that the breeder has recommended and offer this for the first week or two. Make diet changes very gradually to reduce the risk of gastric upsets.

Like babies, puppies grow at an incredibly rapid rate, and they require lots of calories. However, their stomachs are tiny, which is why you should offer several small meals throughout the day, rather than one or two large ones. In the early days your puppy will probably need up to four small feeding a day.

Buy the best quality dog food you can afford and meticulously follow the manufacturer's instructions as to how much and how often to feed. Pet-food manufacturers spend a fortune on researching the correct quantities and ingredients, so take advantage of their work rather than guessing that a couple of spoonfuls is about right.

Age-specific dog foods are available. If you have a puppy, choose a complete food designed to meet the nutritional needs of puppies. These

LEFT: Encourage your children to keep the puppy's water bowls filled with clean water.

OPPOSITE ABOVE: Meeting dogs is an important part of your puppy's training. As an adult, it will have to interact with people and other dogs, and socialization classes are a good way of learning how to do this.

OPPOSITE BELOW: Never allow your children to feed the puppy chocolate, which is poisonous to dogs and can even be fatal.

Child's-eye view
"I think a puppy would like a little bit of chocolate to make him happy."
Sarah Jane, age 5

Tip to parents
Most children love eating chocolate and regard it as a delicious treat, so they are bound to think that dogs will love it too. However, chocolate contains the chemical theobromine, which can be fatal to dogs if consumed in large quantities. As a parent you need to explain that human chocolate is bad for dogs and that the best treat for a puppy is to have someone to play with him and stroke him.

are available as wet or dry formulations. You should continue to offer this food for the first six months to a year before moving to adult dog food.

Drink up!
Access to fresh, clean water is vital. Place more than one bowl of water around the house and encourage your children to fill the bowls daily.

A place of his own
The puppy also needs a safe area — a bed or crate — to which it can retreat. Teach your children to understand that the puppy is not a toy and to respect its personal space and recognize this place as a no-go area (see pages 40–41).

Health
The puppy's first checkup at the vet's office is an ideal time to chat to the vet about deworming, flea and parasite treatments, microchipping and vaccinations (see pages 44–45 and 99–101).

Social work
Ask your vet's office whether they run any puppy socialization classes. If they do, register your puppy. This is a great way for the dog and your family to meet other puppies and owners. By signing your puppy up for a class, you can make a good start on helping it cope with family life and grow into a confident adult dog.

Keeping your dog
happy and healthy

Most families are eager to do as much as they possibly can to look after their dog, but some of these efforts may have an unwanted effect. Explain to the children before the dog's arrival that any form of physical punishment or cruel treatment will have a negative impact on the dog, but also that sometimes, over a lengthy period, too much kindness can be equally distressing.

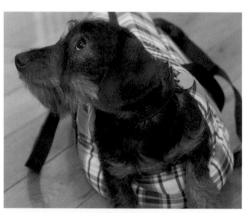

Pampered pooches

In today's celebrity-conscious world, people sometimes want to emulate those socialites who seem to view dogs, particularly toy dogs, as living fashion accessories. Designer fashion houses have waiting lists for their doggy bags, which are basically carryalls used to hold and show off these cute little canines. The trend for carrying puppies and small dogs, rather than allowing them to walk on their own four paws, is now increasingly evident. However, animal welfare societies warn against the practice of carrying dogs everywhere, pointing out that it can be distressing for the animal and that regular opportunities for walking are essential to keep a dog's limbs strong and healthy. There is also a danger that high-strung dogs may find the experience of being taken to loud parties very upsetting, particularly if there is strobe lighting or flash photography.

Sheltered lives

Dogs need plenty of exercise, and bigger, more energetic breeds need lots of access to the outside world. However, all dogs need to be able to shelter from extremes of weather, and that includes heat as well as cold. Dogs are unable to perspire in the same way as humans and can quickly become overheated. The sun can turn a parked car into an oven in a short space of time, so leaving your dog in your car while you do your shopping is very dangerous.

Some hardy breeds can happily live outdoors, provided they have access to a warm, draft-free shelter with a comfortable bed and sufficient food and water. However, older dogs and those with thin coats, such as a Greyhound or Vizsla,

Do!

Provide your dog with appropriate veterinary treatment

Establish routines for meals and exercise sessions

Create opportunities for learning and having fun

Give shelter from the elements

Carry out a socialization program

Don't!

Shout at or hit your dog

Leave it alone so it becomes bored

Isolate it from the family

Allow it to become fat

Carry it everywhere and treat it like a baby

will not be happy staying permanently outdoors and should have their space in the home.

Not a toy

Just because a puppy is small, or a certain breed is classed as a toy dog, it doesn't mean that they are not real dogs. Children must learn to appreciate that such dogs are not toys and should not be carried around like dolls. Encouraging children and dogs to have fun together in ways that allow the dog to engage in normal canine behavior will ensure that everyone remains happy. Even tiny dogs, such as a Chihuahua or Bichon Frise, can enjoy learning basic obedience and doing tricks. They may even be suitable for a sport such as agility.

ABOVE: Your dog needs affection to thrive, but warn your children that it has to be allowed its own space, too.

LEFT: Hardy breeds, such as Huskies and Border Collies, will be content living outdoors, so long as they are fit, young and have suitable shelter.

OPPOSITE: Regular use of doggy bags to carry your puppy is not recommended. Dogs need plenty of exercise to stay healthy.

Lessons in tolerance
for children and dogs

Some family pets are tolerant of children and will stalwartly endure all kinds of indignities, from being dressed up in baby clothes to sitting in the back of wagons and being taken for rides around the neighborhood. However, it is important for children to grasp the concept of respect and not to force any dog to do something that it obviously does not enjoy.

Watch out!

All dogs, no matter how placid they may be, have their breaking point, and children who don't recognize the warning signals can get bitten. Learning to see the world as dogs do and to look for and react to warning signals will help reduce the risk. The signs of canine fear or potential aggression can include:

Wagging the tail in wide, slow sweeps accompanied by growling
Ears straight up
Lips lifted back to reveal teeth
Hackles raised
Dilated, enlarged pupils
Showing the whites of the eyes (when not normally visible)

Question time

Q *I don't think the dog likes me any more. He used to be really cuddly, but now he's just grumpy and growls when I want to give him a hug. Why does he hate me now? Dogs don't suddenly start to hate the people they have previously loved. They could become frightened of them, but if you have not been deliberately cruel to the dog it can be difficult to know exactly why its attitude toward you has changed.*

A Sometimes, when dogs grow older, they don't like as much hugging and handling as they used to do. This may be because their joints and bones are older and more painful, so hugs and cuddles from you may actually be hurting them. The dog can't tell you when something hurts, so it tries to let you know by using other body language, such as growling, biting, trembling or even hiding from you so that you can't find it. We can take the dog to the vet to see if there is anything physically wrong that might explain its behavior. In the meantime, just be patient and kind, and let the dog come to you for attention rather than the other way around.

LEFT: When you are selecting a family pet, choose a breed that will be happy to be cuddled by children.

OPPOSITE: Your child can use treats to help socialize the puppy to any actions, such as opening an umbrella, that it may dislike.

Coping strategies

As soon as your puppy arrives, embark on a socialization program to help it cope with all the different things it may encounter as a family pet (see pages 48–49).

Ideally, the breeder will already have made the puppy familiar with household items, such as the television, radio and vacuum cleaner, and accustomed it to meeting various people. However, don't assume that it is confident with everything and try to introduce it to as many new sights and sounds as possible. Always reward calm behavior and try to ignore any negative reactions as much as possible.

If your dog appears worried by something — the sight of an umbrella being opened, for example — you can encourage your children to help by breaking the movement down into small sections and rewarding the dog with a treat for tolerating each movement. It can be a good lesson for children to learn how to make a dog more confident and to appreciate the importance of patience.

Child's-eye view
"I'd like my dog to do a cartwheel or a roly-poly." Nicole, age 5

Tip to parents
Children have little concept of a dog's physical limitations, and in the world of cartoons, films and books dogs are often portrayed performing human feats. Explain to your child that dogs can't do everything and encourage her to focus on teaching tricks the dog can do, such as roll over or a high-five (see pages 86–89).

chapter 3

The first few days

Now that you and your family have talked through the responsibilities of dog ownership, done your research into the different breeds and decided which puppy you are going to buy, you need to prepare your house for the big day. This chapter will help you get your home ready, buy everything that is required and cope with those all-important first days. Start by stocking up on doggy equipment.

Collar and leash

There is an enormous range of bright, funky designs to appeal to children, but fit and comfort are the most important factors when it comes to choosing a collar. Puppies grow quickly, so don't spend a fortune and buy the best. You can buy a better quality collar once the dog is fully grown.

Have an ID tag engraved with the dog's name and a contact number, and attach this to the collar.

Food and bowls

The best bowls have wide bases and are heavy enough not to tip over. Puppies can chew plastic, so a better choice may be ceramic or metal. A portable, folding water bowl is useful when you are traveling.

Stock up on the food that is recommended by the breeder (see pages 26–27) and store it in a container with a strong lid.

Poop scoops

You can buy eco-friendly paper bags or plastic sacks to pick up dog feces. Dispose of them in accordance with your local bylaws.

Bed and bedding

Initially, a crate, with an adjustable panel that will give the dog more room as it grows, is an ideal, den-like place for the puppy and will also keep it out of trouble. Or a strong cardboard box with a section for the puppy to climb in through can be used.

Place the crate or box in a quiet corner of the puppy's safe room (see page 34) and teach your children to respect this as the puppy's space, which they should leave alone. Line the crate tray with newspaper and provide your puppy with a warm blanket or invest in a specially designed, washable dog bed or beanbag. Charity and thrift stores are good sources of inexpensive towels and blankets.

Grooming gear

Different brushes and combs are available, depending on whether your puppy is a short-, long- or wire-haired breed. Combs with the finest tines are for removing fleas. Stock up on dog shampoo (human shampoos often contain chemicals that will irritate its skin) and keep old towels for drying the puppy after bathing. You will also need dog toothpaste and a dog toothbrush. (See page 52 for more on grooming gear.)

Clicker

This small, plastic device makes a clicking noise when pressed and is used for training. The earlier you start training the better (see pages 76–77). It's a good idea to buy several clickers so that you always have one available.

Toys

Invest in a few toys that your dog can safely chew or play with. Nontoxic materials, such as rubber, are best. Buy toys that are suitable for your puppy's size of mouth.

Creating a
dog-proof
zone

Once you have done your shopping, the next step in your preparations is to make your home as dog-proof as possible. This can be fun for children, who can help you locate potential dangers and spots where little puppies could easily squeeze in and find themselves trapped. Different areas, such as the kitchen, living room and yard, all harbor hidden dangers.

Be safe

Make one room in the house as secure as you possibly can and keep the puppy enclosed there when it first arrives. You can gradually introduce the puppy to other areas of the home as the days go by.

You might want to think about installing a child's stair-gate so that you can block off the puppy's safe room. Later, you can use the gate to keep the puppy off stairways or out of areas you don't want it to go. You may be able to find a second-hand stair-gate in a second-hand store.

Kitchens, which are full of appliances like ovens and dishwashers, are particularly dangerous places for a curious puppy, which may venture too close to a hot oven or be alarmed by the sound of the dishwasher. If there

Question time

Q *What's the best way to pick up the puppy and take him home?*
You will need to arrange a collection date with the breeder. Try to arrive in good time, so that everyone is relaxed. Although your children might want to hold the puppy, it is better to transport it in a secure traveling crate. Take an old sweater or blanket to the breeder a few days beforehand and ask for this to be put into the puppy's bed. When you pick up the puppy, put the sweater in its traveling crate and later in its bed.

A We will have to arrange a time with the breeder and make sure we arrive good and early so that we're all as calm as possible, even though we'll all be really excited. I know you will want to hold the puppy, but we need a proper box or crate to bring it home in. It will feel much better in its box than if it is squeezed in your arms throughout the entire journey. So that it can get used to its new home, we can ask the breeder to put one of your old sweaters in the puppy's bed for a few days before we pick it up. When we get home we can put the sweater in its bed to remind the puppy of its doggy family, so it won't be worried about being in a new place.

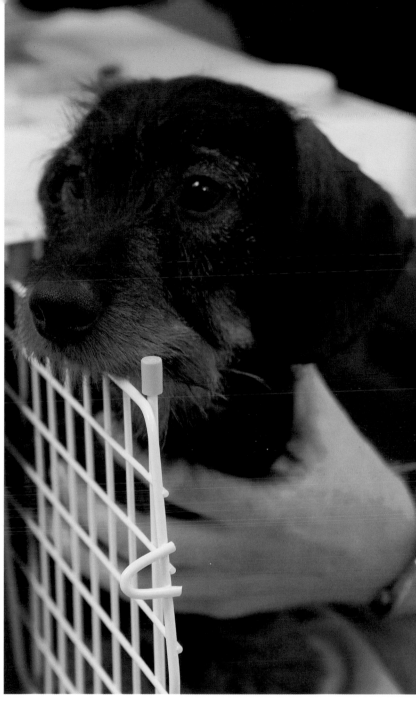

ABOVE: The best way to bring your puppy home is in a secure traveling box or crate, ideally lined with an old sweater that was placed for a few days in the puppy's bed at the breeder's.

OPPOSITE: A child's stair-gate is ideal for preventing your puppy from entering certain areas of the house.

are any gaps under the kitchen cupboards, erect temporary boards until the puppy has grown too big to squeeze underneath.

Check living rooms for dangers such as dangling wires behind electrical equipment, low coffee tables from which a puppy could pull down items, such as cups of hot coffee, and fragile ornaments within paw-reach. Clear up anything that you don't want chewed. If necessary, buy some extra toy boxes with lids, so that children can tidy their toys safely away.

Ask the children to create notes, such as "Check for the puppy," which can be pinned on to the front and back doors. These may help everyone remember to shut the doors and prevent the puppy from escaping. If there is a pet flap, make sure it is locked until the yard has been secured.

Tip to parents
You will already have scheduled the date for the puppy's arrival and your children might enjoy making and decorating a countdown calendar, which they can mark off in anticipation of the big day.

Welcome home
to your new puppy!

Resolve to make your puppy's first few hours and days in its new home as calm and pleasant as possible. This will not always be easy when you have excitable children who are desperate to hold and cuddle it all the time and then start arguing about whose turn it is. It is important to explain to children how frightening their behavior can be to a little puppy.

Preparing the ground

If you discuss beforehand how the puppy might be feeling when it arrives, your children will have a better idea about how they should behave while it is settling into the home. Things to ask your children to consider can include:

How do you think the puppy will feel when it gets here? Will it be happy, sad or frightened?

What sort of things might we do that could scare a puppy?

Will it be missing its mom and its brothers and sisters?

How can we welcome it and make it feel more confident?

Who is going to hold the puppy first? How long will you hold the puppy before it is someone else's turn?

Do you think puppies get tired easily?

Child's-eye view
"I think on the first day my puppy will be so excited it won't be able to sleep." Maisie, age 3

Tip to parents
Children often assume that animals will feel the same emotions as them. Try to explain that the puppy may well be excited, but that it will also be a little overwhelmed by all the noise and confusion and will need lots of naps and quiet time.

How will we know if the puppy is tired?
We need to teach the puppy to pee and poo outdoors, so how are we going to do that and how can you help?

How can we introduce it to all our other pets?

Which room is it going to stay in for the first few days?

What are our house rules going to be for the puppy?

Introductions

If you have other pets, such as another dog or a cat, take time to introduce them slowly and safely. You can put the puppy in a crate and allow the other pet to sniff it. Alternatively, let them meet on neutral territory, with both dogs on leashes. Make lots of fuss of the existing pet so that it doesn't lose confidence or become jealous, and try to maintain its food and exercise routine as much as possible to reassure it that all is well.

ABOVE: Supervise the puppy as it meets your other pets.

BELOW: Ask children to approach the new puppy with respect.

OPPOSITE: Children can help with housebreaking by taking the dog out after a meal.

Question time

Q *Why does my puppy pee everywhere?*
You must expect some accidents, particularly at first when the puppy is getting used to new scents and sounds and has not yet settled into a routine. Little puppies have small bladders and cannot hold urine for very long. The more you show your puppy when and where it should go to relieve itself, the quicker it will learn.

A It's because it's little and doesn't know where it is supposed to go. It's up to us to teach it. We must keep taking the puppy outside when it needs to go, especially after it has just woken up or been fed. When it does go where it is supposed to, don't forget to let the puppy know by telling it what a good dog it is.

Lifting and carrying
a puppy

A puppy that is happy to be lifted and carried is much easier to handle when it grows up. Learning the correct way to lift and carry a dog is essential for building confidence in both puppy and the child. The puppy will want to feel secure and comfortable in your child's arms, and you must judge whether you think your child is capable of holding it securely.

Lifting and carrying a puppy

1 Your child should crouch down and bend his knees, keeping his back straight so he doesn't injure himself when he lifts. He should gather the puppy firmly to him, with one arm around the dog's chest to stop it escaping and the other arm under the puppy's bottom for support. Encourage your child to talk gently to the dog to instill confidence and trust.

2 The puppy should be kept close to his body as the child slowly straightens to an upright position, keeping his back straight, so that the dog feels safe and doesn't jump from his arms. If the puppy feels in danger of being dropped, it will struggle to free itself, so it's important to maintain a secure, but not tight, hold and to keep talking reassuringly.

Dogs aren't toys

Carrying a puppy requires care, thought and a degree of coordination, so it's unwise to let small children lift and carry puppies without proper supervision. Young children aged about six and under have a short attention span (and the younger they are, the shorter it is), so they soon forget not to hug tightly or run with the dog, or they may drop the puppy when they have finished playing with it, as they would a toy.

If such rough handling goes unchecked, the dog will become wary of being picked up and may show aggression, fear or both when someone approaches. What's more, a puppy's bones are delicate and will not develop fully until the dog is a few months old. If your child yanks or pulls at the puppy, it could sustain injuries that will have serious consequences later in life.

Why puppies wriggle

The majority of dogs don't particularly like being picked up and carried, and they will respond by wriggling when people try to do so. This is because dogs feel vulnerable without the use of their legs to run away from danger or defend themselves. If a dog is held firmly or squeezed, its instincts will tell it that it is under threat, and it will naturally try to escape or fight off a perceived attacker. Help your child understand why the puppy struggles and objects when he tries to pick it up or holds it too tightly, so that he doesn't assume that the dog simply doesn't like him.

3 When walking with the puppy, your child should carry the dog close to his chest and be alert for any signs of it tensing up in readiness to try to jump down. To put the puppy down, simply reverse the actions.

Do! encourage your child to …
Support the puppy's bottom
Hold the dog securely to prevent it from jumping free
Talk calmly and reassuringly
Take things slowly

Don't! encourage your child to …
Hug or squeeze the puppy
Shout excitedly while holding the dog
Pick up a dog that's too big
Move abruptly or run when holding a puppy

Too much smother love

All puppies need to sleep a lot, particularly during the day, as this is when they recharge their energy levels and get on with the business of growing. Unfortunately, in a household of lively children it is not always easy to ensure that a young puppy is left alone to enjoy its naps. Make it a golden rule that children should never be allowed to wake the puppy when it is sleeping.

ABOVE: To discourage puppies from developing bad habits, such as tail-chasing and play-biting, allow them to expend any excess energy on a vigorous game with a favorite toy.

OPPOSITE: Puppies need their beauty sleep. Ask your children not to disturb the puppy when it is having a nap, even if this is in the middle of the day.

Let sleeping dogs lie

Ask your children to consider how scared they would feel if they were suddenly or roughly pulled from their beds when they were fast asleep. A tiny puppy will find such an experience just as intimidating and would not be happy to play with them.

When the puppy does wake up, make sure that it has some time when it is not being handled so that it can safely explore its environment and become familiar with the sights and sounds of its new home.

Down time

Just like children, some puppies can become a little overexcited or irritable if they have not had enough sleep. If you think this is happening, it's best to

Tip to parents

Discourage your children from touching the dog when it is sleeping, eating or chewing a rawhide bone. Even though your dog may tolerate this type of treatment, other dogs may not, and your child will be vulnerable to being bitten.

give it a little timeout from all the stimulation in the home. Do this by putting it in its bed or crate where it can experience some quiet time and calm down.

Never scold or be heavy-handed with the puppy when you want it to calm down and be quiet or it will come to perceive being put in its bed or crate as a negative experience. Simply pick the puppy up gently and put it down on its bed – the puppy should soon close its eyes and fall asleep. Always allow your puppy some quiet time after it has eaten so that it is able to digest its food.

Play time

As you get to know your puppy it will quickly become clear when it is likely to be more active. Usually this is in the evenings, although it may well have a "crazy half-hour" during the day when it tears around, chasing its tail or play-biting. Rather than allowing the puppy to develop bad habits, use these active periods to channel its energy more positively. If possible, start to engage it in play a few minutes before a manic moment and introduce games, such as retrieving a toy or playing hide-and-seek with some tidbits of food. By having a lively game or taking it for a walk before bedtime, you will help the puppy to sleep well. Its pre-bedtime walk is also essential to help it become housebroken.

Keeping
the peace

Teaching your children to be gentle and to overcome their feelings of frustration if a puppy doesn't immediately respond to them is an important life lesson. They need to learn to respect the dog, but, at the same time, it's essential that the presence of the new puppy, which will inevitably be the center of attention for a few days or weeks, doesn't make a child feel neglected.

Sibling rivalry

All children are unique in their behavior, and even siblings brought up in the same household can surprise you with the way they react to a new dog in the family. Sometimes a child may become slightly jealous, perhaps if a puppy consistently obeys commands better from another family member. If this happens, try to explain that the puppy is not doing anything on purpose and is not deliberately ignoring her.

You can also help by supervising some quality time between the child and the dog. Give the child some special treats for the dog that can be used in training, and try to teach her how to use clearer commands and signals, so that the puppy learns to come to all members of the family on command or go from a standing position into a sit (see pages 78–81). If you emphasize

Question time

Q *My son is four years old and can sometimes be a little rough with the puppy. How can I stop this?*
If you have a very small child, under the age of six, sit him down comfortably with the puppy and then guide his hands so that he can learn how to stroke and hold the animal. The golden rule should always be "gently does it." Equally, discourage the puppy from becoming overboisterous and engaging in undesirable behavior, such as nipping the child's ankles or fingers. It may be cute in a tiny puppy, but it's less so when the dog is fully grown. Teach your child to say the word "no" and immediately end the game, so that the puppy learns it is much more fun when it plays gently. Equally, stop your child from playing with the puppy if he becomes rough.

A Remember that you must always be gentle with the puppy or it will become frightened and won't want to play with you at all. Let me hold your hand while you stroke it. You can feel how softly we are doing this. If it's any rougher than this, the game will have to end.

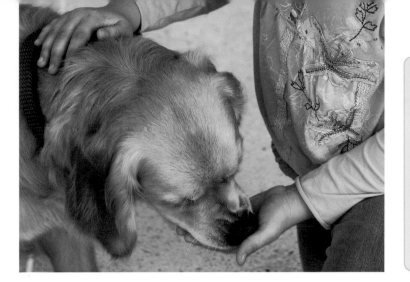

Tip to parents
Avoid arguments about whose turn it is to hold a puppy by investing in an egg-timer or setting the microwave to beep after five or 10 minutes. Children get very upset if they suspect another child is "getting more time." Using a timer will appeal to their sense of fair play and provide an opportunity for the puppy to be put into its bed for quiet time.

the importance of using reward and positive motivation when training, the child should soon enjoy successful results.

No hitting

If a child accidentally or purposefully hits the puppy, the animal will soon lose confidence and be extremely wary of interacting with the child in the future. For this reason, the importance of supervision, particularly with young children whose movements are less coordinated, cannot be overemphasized.

Space invaders

Teach children not to disturb the puppy when it is eating. Ask them to imagine how they would feel if they were just about to sit down to a lovely lunch and someone came up behind them and lifted them right out of their chair. Clearly, this would be irritating, to say the least, and the same applies to your puppy. No matter how good-natured it is, it is important for children to respect its privacy and allow it to eat undisturbed. If a dog is taken away from its food before it has finished it may begin to develop guarding behavior. Left unchecked, this could be dangerous as the dog could start to snap.

ABOVE: If your child has difficulty in getting the dog to obey commands, try giving her some high-value treats (such as pieces of chicken) to use during training.

RIGHT: Make sure each member of the family is giving the dog the same signals and verbal commands for the same actions. If you use different commands, it may become confused.

OPPOSITE: A small child should be shown how to hold and stroke a puppy gently.

Going to
the vet

As soon as possible after picking up your puppy you should arrange for it to visit the vet for a checkup. Even if you think the puppy is in good health, it is useful for the vet to give it a checkup, otherwise some congenital or hereditary problems may go undetected and cause problems later in life.

First visit

Make the first visit as positive an experience as possible for your puppy, using treats and toys before, during and after the occasion. Transport the puppy in its carrier and leave plenty of time to arrive for the appointment early, so that it has a chance to sit in the waiting room and get used to the sights and smells associated with the office. Taking the puppy early will also provide an opportunity for staff members to meet it, and it will enjoy plenty of attention from everyone so that it begins to build positive associations with the vet's office.

Most vets don't mind one or two children being involved in the consultation, but if you have a large family this could be problematic as most consulting rooms are quite small. If you're in doubt, phone the office beforehand.

Your vet will chat with you first to find out whether the puppy has been dewormed and vaccinated (see pages 99–101), what its diet is and so on. You may also be asked about any pre-breeding tests that were carried out on its parents. All this information should have been provided to you by the breeder.

Examining the puppy

For a full clinical examination, you will lift the puppy on to the examination table and hold it steady while the vet looks it over (see right for the different checks that will be made).

If necessary, your vet will prescribe medication against fleas and other parasites, and discuss when you will need to return for vaccinations against viral diseases. You will also get advice on the importance of maintaining regular dental care, neutering, microchipping and any puppy socialization classes that are held at the clinic.

The vet will look into the puppy's ears and eyes, checking that they are clean and healthy.

The mouth, gums and teeth will be examined for signs of soreness, to ensure the dog can eat properly.

A stethoscope will be used to check for potential problems in the puppy's heart and lungs.

Question time

Q *Isn't the vet being mean and hurting my puppy by sticking a needle in him?*
You can explain that there's no need to be concerned as the needles used to vaccinate puppies are small and fine and that the shots are given where the skin is quite thick. Vets love animals and everything they do is done to help them.

A There's honestly no need to worry that the vet is going to hurt the puppy. The needles are so small and fine that the puppy will hardly feel anything at all. The shots are given into parts of the dog where the skin is quite thick. You can always help to cheer up the dog afterward by giving him a special treat and cuddling him.

The vet will look at the coat to determine if there is evidence of flea infestation, which can be common in puppies.

The puppy's back end will be checked for evidence of any diarrhea, soreness or parasite infestation.

Tip to parents

Before your appointment, make a list of any questions you want to ask the vet, such as whether you can change the puppy's diet and how and when you should go about doing this.

The abdomen will be palpated to allow the vet to feel some of the abdominal organs.

Legs and paws will be examined for evidence of joint problems or ingrowing claws.

chapter 4

Routine matters

The quicker you can get your puppy into a routine, the quicker it will settle down. It's important that the whole family works together to help the puppy to get used to its new home. This chapter looks at the main areas in which children can take responsibility for their new pet, from feeding and grooming to helping the puppy fit into its surroundings.

Importance of routine

Puppies are creatures of habit and this can be used to good effect in their training and in helping them settle in quickly. Taking it to the same spot in your yard to pee and poo, for example, will help it learn where you want it to perform, and scheduling these outdoor trips at the same times, after meals and before bed, will reinforce the message. Don't expect housebreaking to be achieved immediately, however; it takes time (see pages 114–15 for information about housebreaking problems).

Dinner time

Establish a dinner-time routine, giving meals at the same time every day, and make sure that play sessions take place after the puppy has eaten. Adopt the same regime as your breeder in the early days: if your puppy is used to four meals a day, continue with this for at least a week or so, before starting a new routine. Puppies are clever and will soon start letting you know if you are late with something. Standing with a food bowl in their mouth is enough of a reminder for most people.

If you have allocated the responsibility for feeding the puppy to your children, it is important to supervise them and make sure that the task is done properly. Help them understand how important it is by asking them to imagine how they would feel if one day mom or dad forgot to give them their breakfast until lunchtime and then woke them up from a nap to give them their dinner or, worse still, forgot to feed them at all. (See pages 50–51 for how your child can be involved in feeding the dog.)

Bedtime

As a parent or guardian you will know the importance of a regular, nighttime routine to help children calm down and fall asleep easily. It is just as important to do this with a puppy, although the technique is slightly different.

Rather than giving the puppy a bath and a bedtime story, you should start the nighttime routine by putting a stop to boisterous games half an hour before you want the puppy to settle down. Take it for a walk, let it go outside and give it a quiet cuddle. Its eyes will begin to close quite quickly as it relaxes, and you can gently put the puppy into its bed. Keeping the bed in a quiet, warm room will stop it from being disturbed by other family activities and noise.

New sights
and sounds

What if your kids never left the house? If they never played with friends or met new people? What if the only people they knew were family? When they did eventually come across strangers they would be wary and fearful. This is what it's like for a new puppy. Coming into a home with all its noises and different creatures can be scary.

About the house

It's important to make the puppy comfortable with the key sights and sounds around the house. Sit down with your child and work out a list of things the puppy should gradually be exposed to. The list might include very regular things such as different rooms, the television, telephone, your child's toys; but don't forget more unusual sounds, such as computer games, the washing machine and the vacuum cleaner.

LEFT AND ABOVE: A home is full of strange noises. Be sure your pooch is familiar with day-to-day sounds in different areas of the house.

OPPOSITE: Take every opportunity to introduce your dog to people who visit your home. It's important to get it used to regular visitors, such as friends, letter carriers or couriers.

Visitors

Don't delay in socialization. Invite regular visitors, relatives and particularly your children's friends. Your kids can take an active role in showing their friends how to behave with a new puppy. Remember that children can be boisterous when they're together, so keep an eye on them. Make sure all new meetings happen close to the dog's bed as this will provide some comforting odors that will relax it.

The dog about town

Socializing a dog is a great project for a child and you can take one thing from your list to do each day of, say, a school vacation, ticking it off on successful completion. Once the dog is fully vaccinated, walks open up a world of new experiences and your children will love showing off the puppy to strangers. Here are some of the people, places and things your dog should meet and greet when out on a walk:

Different people
- [ ] A mixture of ages and ethnicities
- [ ] People walking other dogs
- [ ] Delivery drivers
- [ ] People wearing helmets, hats or carrying walking sticks and umbrellas
- [ ] Joggers
- [ ] Men with beards and/or glasses

Other animals
- [ ] Other dogs
- [ ] Cats
- [ ] Livestock (cattle, pigs, sheep)
- [ ] Horses

Vehicles
- [ ] Cars
- [ ] Bicycles
- [ ] Motorcycles
- [ ] Buses
- [ ] Trucks

Environments
- [ ] Friends' houses
- [ ] Shopping centers
- [ ] Playgroups
- [ ] Parks
- [ ] Obedience classes
- [ ] Schoolyard
- [ ] Countryside

Question time

Q *Why does my dog always pee on posts? This is a common question as it is a behavior pattern that is so foreign to a child's sensibilities. It's a dog's instinct to mark its territory through urine and to "overmark" other dogs' scent trails.*

A He does it because he's marking his territory. He's leaving a calling card to tell other dogs who he is, that he's a boy and that he lives in this area. See how he sniffed the post first? What's probably happened is that another dog has marked it first and now Charlie is overmarking.

Q *Why does he smell other dogs' bottoms? This is another behavior pattern that will be alien to your child. The olfactory system of dogs is their primary source of investigation. They can learn many things from one sniff when greeting a fellow canine, including the other dog's general health and if a female pooch is sexually healthy. A dog's anal glands are also located here and carry the dog's individual scent.*

A Sniffing is a dog's way of saying hello and finding out about another dog. There's more to it than just sniffing though. Look how they bump each other first. They're finding out who's the bigger and who will be the boss. It sets the rules for the play that will follow.

Child's-eye view
"I think a puppy might be scared at night, when it's dark, because he's missing his mom." Lily, age 7

Tip to parents
Putting a blanket that smells of his mother in the puppy's basket will help comfort him at night.

Getting some
food for thought

Puppies are usually introduced to solid food when they are about three weeks old. By the time you get your dog, usually between seven and 10 weeks old, it will be eating four small meals a day. You can gradually reduce this to three by about 12 weeks of age and then two feedings at four or five months old. Adult dogs need one or two meals a day, which can be moist or dry.

All change

When you first get your puppy, it is advisable to feed it the same food that the breeder was offering. Stock up on supplies before you bring the puppy home and maintain the diet for the first few weeks. After that time, make any changes very gradually to avoid the risk of gastric upset. In addition, ensure your dog has fresh water at all times.

Balanced diet

Dry "complete" dog foods are designed to provide a nutritionally balanced diet. However, some foods may not be nutritionally complete and may require additional supplements. Check the label to find out what the food provides. A diet composed solely of moist foods may also require dry supplements in order to keep your dog's teeth in good condition; dry foods are good for oral health as they are abrasive on the teeth when eaten. Ask your vet for advice if you have any concerns about feeding.

Greedy guts

Dogs can be greedy and will eat just about anything, whether it is good for them or not. In addition, children are often guilty of feeding treats from the table, particularly things they do not want to eat themselves. This encourages begging and will add extra calories to the puppy's diet. If you occasionally give the dog a special treat, feed it after your own meal and serve it directly into its dish.

Can I help?

Involve your children in the dog's feeding regime to help them develop a sense of responsibility and to allow the dog to build positive associations. If the children take turns to present the dog food in a dish, they will become popular. Very young children can help by getting the dish or spooning food into it, although you should always keep an eye on how much they put in the dish.

Manners!

It is dangerous for dogs to snatch food, particularly from children, so teach your dog to be patient and to wait for permission. This also reinforces the concept that it is not the leader of the pack and that children must be respected. You should supervise feeding times.

Question time

Q *Urgh! Why does my dog keep on passing wind?*
It could be because you are feeding him too many treats. Foods containing sugar, salt or garlic can all have this effect. Stick to a complete dog food and only feed healthy snacks, such as rawhide chews or carrot sticks. If the problem continues you should seek veterinary advice.

A It's probably having difficulty digesting its food. Some dogs have problems if they eat too many treats or human food. From now on, let's try to feed it nothing but dog food and a few healthy treats to see if that helps.

Q *Why does my dog sometimes eat grass and make itself sick?*
No one really understands why dogs do this, although one theory is that the dog is seeking extra roughage. As you have observed, grass is a natural emetic, so to avoid a mess indoors keep the dog outside until it has vomited. If you are worried, check with your vet.

A Lots of dogs do this. If the dog has eaten something that's made him feel poorly it might eat the grass to help throw up and get rid of it.

Feeding your dog

1 With the bowl of food in one hand, your child should approach the dog and ask it to sit. She should then crouch down and put a hand on its collar before placing the bowl a little distance in front of the dog.

2 The child should give the "wait" command (see pages 80–81), putting the dog back into a sit if it breaks into a stand.

3 When the dog has relaxed into a sit and made eye contact with the child, it is time to give a release command, such as "get it", so that the dog can eat the food. Getting the food is the reward for showing self-control.

A puppy's big brush off

Grooming should be a fun experience for your puppy and something everyone enjoys doing. Try to groom the dog every day so that it gets used to being handled. Demonstrate to your children how to be gentle, particularly if you have a long-haired dog, and if necessary remind them of the fuss they make having the tangles removed from their own hair.

Can I help?

Small children will have difficulty controlling a wriggling puppy and managing a brush at the same time. Don't let your child groom her dog unsupervised; an older child or adult should hold the puppy while the younger child gently brushes it. Make sure children wash their hands carefully after grooming.

If a child thinks she has found a flea while grooming the dog, she should first check what it is with an adult. You can tell it's a flea, rather than just a speck of dirt, because flea dirt contains congealed blood and will dilute to a pinkish color if you put it on a piece of damp cotton batting. Remove the flea from the flea comb with a paper towel and dispose of it in the household garbage (see pages 100–101 for more on removing fleas).

Make grooming sessions short, giving lots of verbal praise, and follow it up with a treat or a game for the puppy so it thinks that grooming is enjoyable. Getting your dog used to being picked up and put on a table to be groomed will help it cope when visiting the vet.

Essential gear

Your dog's coat type will determine the equipment you need, but you will need some, if not all, of the following:

Slicker brush Great for removing dead hair and debris from dense, short coats or curly coats, but if used roughly it can pull and irritate the skin.
Bristle and pin brush Ideal for most short-haired breeds.
Grooming mitts These can be used to help remove dead hair and dirt and to polish the coat.
Steel comb and flea comb These will remove tangles, fleas and ticks.
Cotton batting Useful for cleaning the dog's eyes. Work gently, always wiping outward, and use separate damp pads for each eye.
Scissors If you don't take your dog to a professional dog groomer, scissors may be required for occasional hair trimming. Always use sharp, good-quality scissors with round ends so that you don't accidentally nick the skin.
Nail clippers Use clippers only if you can do the job properly; ask your vet to demonstrate first.
Dog toothbrush and dog toothpaste See pages 56–57 for a guide to cleaning your dog's teeth.

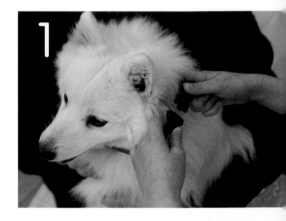

Grooming

1 Before your child begins grooming, put down an old blanket or towel or some newspapers for the puppy to stand on, and take off its collar.

2 The child should begin by brushing with long, smooth strokes from head to tail, combing out any matted fur. You should cut out any mats with scissors if necessary. She can use a flea comb to check for fleas or ticks.

Question time

Q *Why does my dog smell so bad?*
Some dogs are better than others at cleaning themselves, and you may have to resort to regular bathing and to keeping the coat clipped. An older dog may have developed stiff joints or back pain that makes it difficult to clean itself. Bitches are more likely than dogs to get urine on the hair. Clipping around this area *may help. There could be medical reasons, including a discharge from the anal glands, so have the dog checked by a vet.*

A Now that it's getting a bit older it can't clean itself as well has it used to. Perhaps we need to help by clipping its coat. Let's ask the vet for advice.

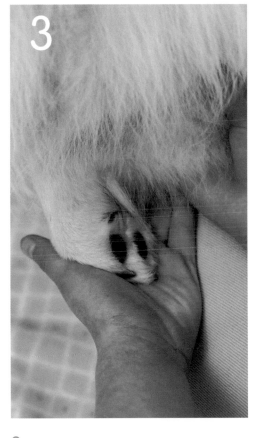

3 Encourage your child to examine the puppy's feet to check for cuts or gravel in its pads.

4 If necessary, you or your child can gently wipe the eyes clean. You should check the puppy's ears and if necessary clean them gently with damp cotton batting. Finally, put on the puppy's collar and give it a hug and a treat.

Time for a bath
and some fun!

Just like children, some dogs take special delight in getting themselves as dirty as possible when they're out playing. Even if you don't show your dog it will be necessary to bathe it occasionally, and if it suffers from a skin allergy or develops fleas your vet may prescribe a special shampoo. Bathing helps remove dead hair and debris from the coat, making the puppy smell a lot fresher.

Soap stars

There is a huge range of canine shampoos, for different breeds and coat types and colors. Puppies need a mild puppy shampoo that will not irritate their skin. Don't use human shampoo or dishwashing liquid on your dog, as these may irritate its skin or contain chemicals that could be toxic if it licks its coat. You can also buy coat conditioners to apply after the shampoo and make your dog's coat soft and shiny, but rinse these out properly with warm, clean water.

Professional dog groomers have hairdriers on stands that circulate air over the dog while it is in a cage. However, an ordinary hairdrier will do the job just as well, as long as it has heat controls so that you can select the coolest setting.

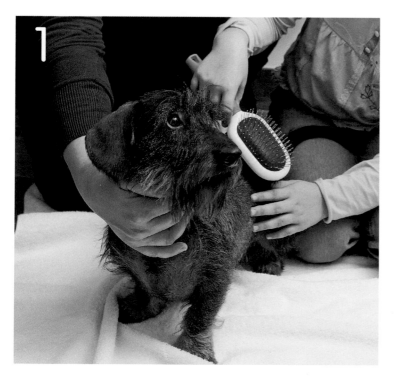

Bathing your dog 1 Fill the bath with warm, tepid water, testing with an elbow just as you would for a baby. Put down towels for the dog to stand on and have towels ready to dry it with. Your child can help by brushing the dog thoroughly to remove as many dead hairs as possible.

2 Gently lift the dog into the water. Use a jug to pour water on the coat, being careful not to get water in its eyes or ears.

How often?

Bathe your dog as often as needed, but generally not more than once a month. Bathing too often removes the natural oils from the coat, and these are needed to keep the dog warm and dry. Older dogs and those with thinner coats should be bathed less often than young, boisterous dogs or those with thick, dense coats.

Can I help?

If the weather is hot, it can be fun to bathe the dog outside. Children love hosing off the dog, but always supervise this to make sure that no water goes into the dog's eyes or ears. In colder weather, you will have to bathe the dog indoors, either in the sink, using a hose attachment, or in the bathtub. You will probably need to restrain the dog yourself during bathing (putting a nonslip mat on the bottom of the bath will help the dog to grip and be easier to handle), but your child can help with the preliminary brushing and drying afterward.

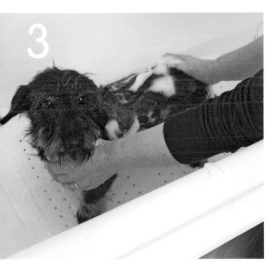

3 Apply dog shampoo by putting a small amount on your hand or using a sponge and lathering well. Massage the shampoo gently into the dog's fur. Rinse all the suds away and, if necessary, apply conditioner before rinsing again.

4 Lift the dog out and wrap it quickly in a towel. Ask your child to rub the dog down with the towel. If your dog will accept a hairdrier, use it on the lowest setting and move it in swift, wide movements over the dog's body to avoid scorching.

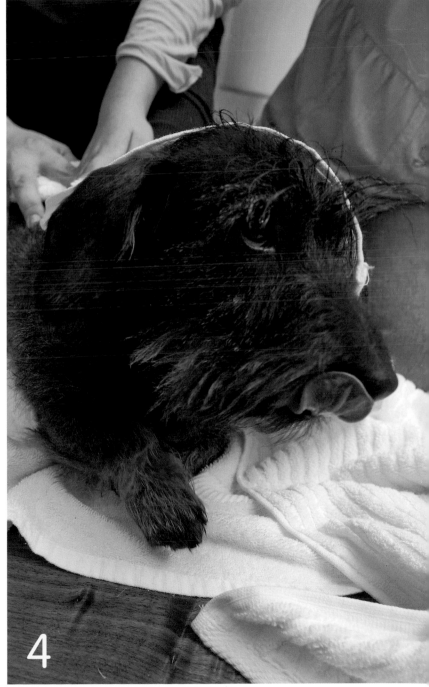

Checkups
from nose to tail

If you get into the habit of giving your dog a daily or weekly health check you will spot problems much more quickly than if you wait for him to develop noticeable symptoms. You'll also get him used to being handled in a similar way to how a vet will examine him. This is important for all dogs, but particularly large ones, who are more difficult to deal with if they refuse to be examined.

Keeping an eye on him

You will probably want to take responsibility for checking your dog's health yourself, but you can ask your child to help you, perhaps by stroking and reassuring the dog as you check it. A good time to do a health check is before and during grooming sessions. Lift the dog onto a table, standing it on a nonslip mat or damp towel so it doesn't slip. Afterward, reward the puppy with verbal praise and a treat before lifting it gently down onto the floor. You should check for the following:

> **Lumps, bumps or injuries** Run your hands from head to tail to look for any problems.
> **Scruff and armpits** Look for signs of fleas and ticks here and elsewhere.
> **Gums and teeth** Wear gloves to check for missing teeth and signs of dental decay. Lift the dog's lips and run your fingers inside its gums and teeth. The dog's gums should be nice and pink.
> **Eyes** Look at the eyes for signs of discharge and infection.
> **Ears** Examine the ears to make sure they look and smell clean and healthy.
> **Feet** Check for cuts or impacted gravel. Examine its claws to make sure they are not too long or ingrowing.

Down in the mouth

Some 85 percent of adult dogs exhibit signs of gum disease. Teeth brushing is the way to prevent this, and the younger your puppy is when you start to get it used to it, the easier it will be. You

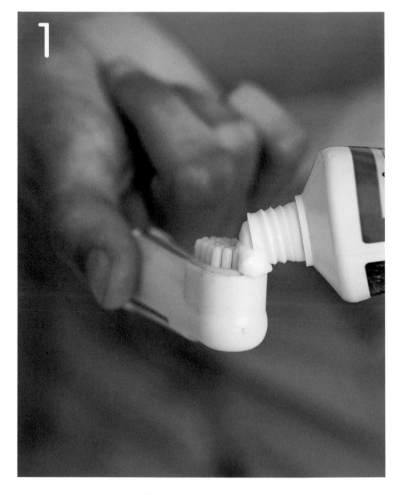

Cleaning your dog's teeth

1 Ask your child to put a tooth-cleaning tip on a finger (or wear a rubber glove) and add a small blob of dog toothpaste.

could hold the dog's head while an older child brushes, but it's probably best to do the brushing yourself if the child is young.

Is his nose wet?

Some scientists believe that moisture helps to make a dog's nose more sensitive to smells, while others think that the wetness and evaporation act as a cooling mechanism. Either way, a healthy dog normally has a wet nose, and illness can dry it out and make it feel hot. However, if there are no other signs of illness, a warm, dry nose may not be sufficient reason to rush off to the vet.

Signs that your dog may be unwell

Consult your vet if any of the symptoms in this checklist gets worse or lasts for longer than 24 hours.

- [ ] Loss of appetite
- [ ] Excessive drinking
- [ ] Vomiting or diarrhea
- [ ] Inability to pass urine
- [ ] Constipation
- [ ] Self-harm, such as chewing or excessive licking
- [ ] Dull coat

- [ ] Limping
- [ ] Head shaking
- [ ] Offensive smell
- [ ] Runny eyes or nose
- [ ] Coughing or excessive panting

2 The child should very carefully pull back the dog's lip and use the tip to gently rub toothpaste over the dog's teeth. If the dog does not like the feel of a pet toothbrush, the toothpaste can be applied with a glove-covered finger.

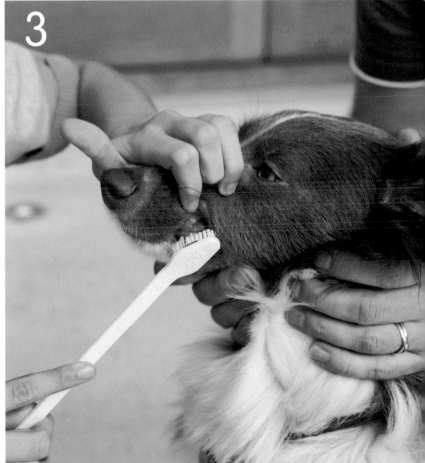

3 A longer toothbrush can also be used, for easy access to the back teeth. Make sure that children never try to clean a dog's teeth with their own toothbrush!

Having fun at
puppy playtime

Puppies learn a great deal from play, and it is a crucial part of their development. When they play with other dogs and puppies they learn how to relate to their own kind, read body language, use their teeth softly and cope with different sizes and breeds of dog. When they play with children and other family members, they should learn how to be confident but not overboisterous.

Stay safe

Take into account your dog's breed when it is playing with your children. Too much rough-housing or tug-of-war-style games can over-excite dogs, and they may become dangerous, particularly if they are larger breeds. Using toys, such as a ball or Frisbee, can help to exercise the dog and develop its coordination, and the toys can be used to start training it. Chasing games can overstimulate dogs such as Border Collies, so channel their energies into something more constructive, such as negotiating obstacles and catching a ball and bring it back again.

A puppy's teeth can be needle sharp and will hurt if they are allowed to play-bite. A puppy often bites to relieve gum discomfort when new teeth are coming through, so providing teething toys to chew on will help to discourage it from biting a nearby arm or leg. Thankfully, most puppies grow out of play-biting by the time they are about 20 weeks.

Come back!

Encourage your children to hide treats around the house or yard for the dog to find. Let it see them hiding them at first, but then make it more difficult by putting the dog in another room.

ABOVE: Terriers love soft toys — perfect for hunting down and "killing"!

OPPOSITE ABOVE: Your child's relationship with the puppy can be strengthened if a favorite toy is reserved for her alone to offer to it.

OPPOSITE BELOW: Encourage your puppy to become a sleuth. Your child can hide a tasty treat in the corner of the house or yard and watch the pup track it down.

Tip to parents
You don't have to spend a fortune on toys for your puppy. A strong plastic lid can make a good substitute Frisbee, or visit your local second-hand store to find some cuddly soft toys.

Question time?

Q When can I play with my dog?
It's important to give your dog at least half an hour to digest its food before you allow your children to play with it. Two or three short play sessions scheduled throughout the day are better for dogs than one long, exhausting game, particularly for very young or old dogs, who may be prone to injuries or aches and pains.

A Wait for half an hour after its meal so that it can let its food go down properly. Dogs like lots of short games rather than one big long one, which might be tiring if it's only a baby or very old.

Ask the children to hide while you hold the dog, and then let go with the command "find". When the dog finds its young owner it can be rewarded with a treat. These are good training games and can help the puppy get to know its name and assist with the recall command. Associating returning to someone when called and then receiving a treat or lavish praise and attention will reinforce the idea that humans are fun, and you will not experience problems trying to get the dog to come back to you when you call it (see pages 78–79).

It is important to remind children that not every game will be appropriate. Hide-and-seek, treasure hunts and obstacle races are all perfect, but activities like climbing trees and skateboarding are beyond the ability of most dogs! (See pages 90–91 for more ideas for games to play.)

Getting ready to
walk this
way

Walking is a great way for the family to get fit together and will help strengthen the relationship between you and your dog. It's also an ideal opportunity to practice some socialization and training techniques. Encourage your children to accompany you on walks as much as possible, even in bad weather, so that they develop a sense of responsibility and commitment.

Tip to parents
Invest in some high-visibility rainwear or warm weather clothing so that your children are easily seen but remain dry and warm. High-visibility dog coats, leashes and collars will help make winter walking safer for your dog.

Get the kids out there
Taking a regular part in dog walking will help strengthen your children's relationship with the puppy, and at the same time contribute to keeping them healthy. They will enjoy taking turns at holding the dog's leash, and you can give them treats and toys to reward the dog for coming when called. Other responsibilities can be allocated, such as carrying the dog's water bottle or cleaning up after the puppy (see opposite).

Question time

Q *I don't want to walk. I want to go and play with my friends.*

Dogs need to walk regularly every day to exercise and keep their joints fit and healthy. If children want the fun of owning a dog, they must understand the importance of this. You can take toys and treats with you on the walk and play games when you are out so that the dog and child have fun together. Try inviting your child's friends along on the walk and making a list of things to spot along the way, such as a particular type of tree, a flower or a local landmark. Make it a game for the children to find these items and tick them off on a list. If you make the walks fun experiences, your child will soon discover the joy of the great outdoors and the thrill of finding out just what makes the puppy happy.

A The dog will be sad if you don't walk it. It will also not be very healthy because it needs lots of walking to keep fit. Imagine if you were stuck indoors all the time, forced to watch the rest of the family playing. Why don't we invite some of your friends to come along, too. Can you think of some games we could all enjoy together? How about a treasure hunt?

ABOVE: Picking up feces with a plastic bag over the hand is the easiest way of cleaning up after your dog.

FAR LEFT: A walk in the park with the dog is a wonderful way of spending time together as a family.

LEFT: A high-visibility collar and leash make your dog safer in low-light conditions.

How far should we go?

How far you walk and how often will largely depend on the type of dog you have. Some of the working and pastoral breeds require more exercise than the smaller dogs, but even a Yorkshire Terrier is capable of enjoying quite a lengthy walk as long as it is fit and healthy.

The amount of exercise a dog needs will change over the years, and an older dog may gradually become reluctant to walk very far. However, gentle, frequent walks will help to keep the dog mobile and fit, so pop a warm coat on it and encourage it to join you outside despite any misgivings.

When you are walking puppies, try to plan the route so that at least half the walk is off hard ground. This will protect their pads and joints from overexertion.

Clean up!

It is an antisocial act for dog owners not to clean up after their dogs, particularly when there are children in the area. Dog feces can contain bacteria that can be transmitted to children, either through direct contact or indirect contact, such as touching their shoes, which have been contaminated through walking in waste matter.

Kennel clubs encourage children over the age of eight to be involved in picking up dog poo, so don't get your children used to the idea that this is something only adults do. When you go out, arm yourself with plastic bags or paper towels to pick up after your dog. Dispose of waste according to your local bylaws, but never put dog feces on garden compost heaps because parasites can contaminate the compost.

chapter 5

Growing pains

Puppies have much in common with children. They love to enjoy themselves and express their joy at the simple things in life, and they are also sometimes naughty. This chapter looks at how you can involve your child in training a puppy, and how you can deal with bad behavior from both the dog and your children.

A dog's world

Dogs can be confused by what children want them to do, particularly if they shriek when they are excited and call the dog's name repeatedly. Teaching your children to read canine body language will enable them to understand how your dog communicates and help to make them safer around all dogs, because they will know how to read the signals that a dog is feeling fearful or defensive (see pages 64–65).

To help your children understand how a dog thinks, ask them to pretend to be a dog and imagine how the world will look from a dog's point-of-view. Remind them that a dog cannot use words to tell us how it is feeling, but must rely on other communication skills. It will use its eyes and highly developed senses of smell and hearing to help it work out whether something is friendly or likely to taste good and whether it recognizes someone. To communicate that it is happy or sad, a dog will use its tail, body language, facial expression, hackles and voice.

Pack animals

Dogs generally adore the company of people, so to be isolated from family life for long periods is something that will make them miserable. Unfortunately, untrained dogs are such a nuisance that they are often kept apart from the family, which exacerbates their behavior problems.

In the wild, dogs are pack animals, and they need to be able to cooperate with each other in order to survive. However, our canine companions don't always understand what we expect from them, so it is important to explain as clearly as possible. For example, if you give the command "down" when you want the dog to jump off a chair or stop jumping up at someone, and then give the "down" command when you want it to lie down, you will confuse it. How can it know whether you want it to jump down off the chair or lie down and get comfy? To avoid confusion, use clear, separate commands, such as "down" when you want it to lie down and "off" when you want it to get off a chair.

Can you tell how a dog feels?

A closer look at your dog's body language will reveal many clues about how it is feeling. As the whole family gets to know the dog, it will become obvious when it is feeling relaxed and when it is nervous or alarmed. Discuss the signs with your children so they do not try to play with the dog when it is not in the mood.

ABOVE: A dog lying on its side with legs extended is feeling tired, but relaxed and secure in its surroundings.

OPPOSITE: If your child looks at the puppy while stroking it or giving a treat, the dog will learn that eye contact with her is not a threat.

Tip to parents
Spending time as a family observing your dog when it is happy will help you to recognize those times when it is feeling less confident or threatened by a new and unpredictable situation.

Body language
If the dog is happy and relaxed its eyes will appear soft, not particularly wide and staring, and it will not show the whites of its eyes (unless, of course, they are always visible). Its ears will be relaxed — that is, neither directly upright nor flat down. When it lies down, its legs will probably be stretched out to the side, showing that it is happy to lie in this vulnerable position rather than defensively, with its legs tucked underneath, ready to leap up and run.

The tail of a happy, relaxed dog is usually up and wagging confidently from side to side as your child plays and interacts with it. It is the human equivalent of shaking your hand when he meets you. A dog that bows toward its owner, with its front end down and back end up in the air, as it wags its tail and perhaps barks, is usually asking for someone to please play a game with it.

If your dog is worried, perhaps because it has met a strange dog for the first time, its tail may be clamped down between its legs. However, if the dog is feeling aggressive it may fluff up its tail, holding it up and straight out, and it may also raise its hackles, lift its lips and growl intermittent warnings, and make staring eye contact.

Do! Encourage your child to …

Observe her dog and try to guess how it's feeling

Understand how a dog communicates

Recognize that confused dogs can give out mixed messages

Get the dog to look at her when they are playing together or she is offering a treat

Say the dog's name only once when she asks it to do something

Don't! encourage your child to …

Assume she knows exactly how a dog is feeling

Make prolonged eye contact with a strange dog

Shout a dog's name repeatedly

He's smiling!

Children always think that smiling means that someone is pleased to see them. If they see a dog curling its lips, they may assume that it is happy to see them. However, this is not always the case. In the dog world, it can mean that the dog is feeling a little uncertain. Some breeds of dog, such as a Doberman and many of the terriers, have a reputation for smiling. Their lips curl up and they show their teeth when they see you so that they do, indeed, look happy. In some cases, this kind of smiling is a sign of submission. However, it is not an aggressive act and there is nothing to worry about.

Working for
treats and rewards

To help your dog learn to behave well among children and other dogs and to adapt to family life, it is important to develop a positive, reward-based training system. Children are familiar with the concept of rewards for work that has been well done, but they are not always certain how to reward their dog. Special toys and healthy treats are much better than things like sweets and cookies.

Food

Dogs are greedy creatures, and food treats are always welcome. Try to get into the habit of offering treats only for work well done, so that they retain their importance. If you or your child offer treats from a plate just because the dog is asking, you will be rewarding it for begging, and there will be less significance attached to the rewards given during training.

Small pieces of cooked sausage, chicken, liver, cheese and tasty dog treats are all suitable rewards in training. Avoid using high-calorie human food, because these will disrupt your dog's calorie intake and lead to weight gain. When you are training your dog and using a lot of treats, remember to factor this into its daily calorie intake to make sure it isn't consuming too many.

Toys

Experiment to see what types of toys motivate your dog most. It may prefer squeaky, noisy toys, a ball or hoop or tug-of-war toys, so experiment to find out which are the favorites. Keep one or two in a special place, out of reach from the dog, to use as rewards. Only allow access to these toys for short periods when the dog has behaved particularly well.

Playtime

Another reward that your dog will appreciate is time off from work to simply play and have fun. Separate training and socialization sessions by scheduling short bursts of play, such as throwing and retrieving a ball or Frisbee. This kind of interactive play, involving your children, will help to teach the dog respect and self-discipline as it learns not to engage in chasing or play-biting.

ABOVE: Dogs love a quick snack and will be all the more eager to obey commands if they know treats are around!

OPPOSITE ABOVE: For maximum effect, find out which toys motivate your dog most.

OPPOSITE BELOW: Sometimes a stroke and a cuddle is just what your dog wants.

Child's-eye view
"I think my dog would like a cookie if he behaved well." Melissa, age 7

Tip to parents
Providing healthy treats (rather than cookies) means that edible rewards can be given more frequently without damaging your dog's health.

Question time

Q *How can I let my dog know when its done something well?*
There are several different types of rewards, and it is important to give them each time the dog does something well to encourage a particular behavior and motivate it to repeat it. In the early days of helping your children to become potty-trained you would give plenty of verbal praise every time they asked to go or successfully passed a dry night. It is the same with dogs: reward even the smallest of breakthroughs, particularly for complicated tasks.

A You get stickers and stars at school, but dogs need different rewards, such as toys, treats and lots of praise in a happy voice. When we are training it to do something we need to give it lots of rewards every time it gets it right, then we can gradually give it less.

Good dog!

One of the most effective rewards is verbal praise, stroking and a generally positive reaction. All this fuss is a cheap, no-calorie technique, guaranteed to make your dog happy. Teach your children to adopt a happy, excited tone when they are praising the dog and a sterner, deeper tone to discourage it. Remind them that dogs have a limited understanding of words and that the tone of voice is always more important. A simple "good dog" is much more effective than a lengthy description of what it has done right.

Teach children that rewarding a dog for good behavior can help to ensure that it behaves well in the future. The dog doesn't have to be doing anything spectacular to be praised. It is also useful to praise it simply for being calm in certain situations, such as when another dog walks past. When a dog does not behave in the way a child wants it to, it is important not to resort to shouting or hitting as this will merely confuse the dog and make it less likely to respond. Show the child how to use distraction with toys or treats to refocus the dog's attention.

Dogs
behaving badly

Every family is different, and no puppy can be expected to know what your rules are and how they are expected to behave. Children learn through observation, so try to behave positively toward your dog. If your children see you acting roughly with the dog, hitting or dragging it, they will assume that this is acceptable behavior and copy you in the future.

Just say "no"

If dogs are not adequately stimulated and are not taught by their owners how to override some of their natural instincts, they can be labeled as naughty or bad for having failed to live up to the family's expectations. Many of these dogs end up in shelters where they can be difficult to rehome. Sadly, the saying that everyone gets the dog they deserve contains more than a grain of truth, and it is usually the case that a so-called naughty dog has been let down by its family.

When a dog is allowed to assume the role of pack leader it will try to assert its dominance. Although this may be quite cute in smaller dogs it can be downright stressful in large, adolescent or adult dogs, who will try to hog the sofa, guard

Tip to parents
Avoid physical punishment because the dog will lose confidence in people and may, through fear, react in an aggressive or defensive way. Ignore unwanted behavior as much as possible, using distraction techniques or timeouts when needed.

Question time

Q *Help! I can't get my dog off my leg! Even worse, he does it to my friends and neighbors too.*

Talk to your vet, as it may help to get your dog neutered. Anesthetics and veterinary techniques have improved so much in recent years that this can be done in puppies as early as eight weeks, and it will greatly reduce his sexual urges. You will also benefit him by making him less frustrated and less likely to roam in search of a mate, thereby reducing his vulnerability to road accidents. Both male and female dogs who have not been neutered are at high risk of infections and some cancers. Mounting can also be a sign of dominance, and taking steps to make sure the dog realizes he is at the bottom of the family hierarchy will help.

A Sometimes a dog will do this when he does not respect you or does not regard you as being in charge of him. We need to make sure that he knows that he is at the bottom of our family pack by making our house rules clear to him. Dogs who have not had a type of surgery called neutering, which makes them unable to breed (have babies), can get frustrated at not having a mate, and jumping up on your leg is one way of letting us know about this. We need to make an appointment with the vet to arrange for our dog to have the operation.

ABOVE: If you let your dog lie on the sofa, you may be storing up trouble for later years. A mature dog's habits are much more difficult to change!

OPPOSITE: Remove the puppy as soon as you spot it in a forbidden area of the house.

LEFT: Your child should simply stop play and walk away if the dog's behavior becomes unacceptable.

their food dishes, sleep in the best places and indulge in antisocial or sexual behaviors, such as constantly attempting to mount someone's leg. If this type of behavior is left untreated it can become so ingrained that the intervention of a professional pet behavior counselor will be required. To prevent this difficult situation from arising, make sure that everyone in the family learns how to effectively say "no" to the dog, and if necessary implement a timeout system so that it has an opportunity to calm down and realize that rough play means no play.

Zero-tolerance
Adopting a zero-tolerance attitude to rough play, chasing, snapping or biting is particularly important when there are children in the family. Under supervision, teach your children to say "no" and to walk away from a dog who is indulging in behavior such as tugging at their clothes or nibbling their toes.

Any further interaction with the dog may be interpreted as part of a huge game, so after you have said "no" simply remove the dog from the situation, perhaps by putting it on its bed or in a different room. If you do this every single time, it will soon get the message that it is much more fun to be sociable and to play gently.

Dealing with
tantrums
and tears

Young children — and some older children, too — can be prone to temper tantrums, often caused by frustration at not getting what they want. Sometimes they rail at something they perceive to be unfair. A toddler is likely to be enraged if another child takes a favorite toy from them, for example, and they may react in a similar way if their dog does the same thing.

Keep your eyes open

Unfortunately, reason often goes out of the window during a tantrum, and the child may resort to violence if the dog takes a favorite toy, perhaps picking up another toy and whacking the dog over the head. It is important to protect your dog from these outbursts, because no matter how good-natured a dog is it will have a mental breaking point. Some dogs will react with fear, running away and hiding from the child, whereas others may react by snapping and biting, which is, of course, dangerous.

The importance of supervision cannot be overstated. Young children are at eye-contact level and their faces are vulnerable. If a tense situation

Do!

Supervise children and dogs constantly
Teach patience
Ask children to tidy up toys, particularly small ones that could be swallowed
Deal promptly with tantrums by removing the child from the situation
Explain the consequences of tantrums and how this could make the dog react

Don't!

Set a bad example to your child by using physical punishment
Allow the dog access to some children's toys and not others
Give the dog old shoes, socks or items of clothing to chew — it will not be able to differentiate between these and new clothes

develops, remove the child as soon as possible, and then turn your attention to the dog, perhaps by trying to retrieve the toy it has grabbed by distracting it with one that it is allowed to have.

Coping with frustration

Owning a dog helps young children learn the concept of patience, and is a good way of encouraging them to develop strategies to cope with frustration. Even very small children must learn that it is never acceptable to hit out at a dog, pull its ears, poke it or in any way be violent. Adopt a zero-tolerance attitude to this, and take the child to a safe, dog-free room. However, it is important to explain why such behavior is unacceptable and the possible dangerous consequences, and then try to think of better and safer ways for the child to deal with frustration — perhaps by coming to find an adult to deal with the situation properly.

ABOVE: Encourage your child to keep all her toys tidied away, so that the dog doesn't become confused about which toys belong to it.

OPPOSITE: Any dog can bite if sorely provoked. All interactions between young children and dogs should be supervised, to ensure that tempers do not fray.

Question time

Q *My dog is really stupid. He won't come when I call him!*
Children can get frustrated if a dog doesn't do something for them, particularly if it does it immediately for another family member.

A He's not being stupid. It's a bit like when I ask you to get ready for school in the mornings and you're busy doing something else, like daydreaming, playing on the computer, watching television or generally feeling too tired or bored. There are lots of reasons why a dog won't do as it is told, but the more we can make training fun for it the better it will do.

chapter 6

Training for kids

This chapter shows how children can be involved in all aspects of training, from the basics needed for good canine behavior to advanced tricks, such as jumping through hoops. Start training your dog early. The sooner it learns how to respond to its name, to come when called and to sit or lie down on command, the more you can enjoy having it as a family member. Make sure everyone in the family uses the same basic commands so that the dog isn't confused.

Standing tall

If you have chosen a large breed, young children will often be smaller than the dog when it reaches adulthood. Standing taller than another dog or pinning another dog down is one of the ways that dogs determine who is the more dominant. It is important to start training as a puppy so that this does not become a problem. If you have a large dog, sit the child on your knee and encourage him to pet the dog from this elevated position. Always discourage rough play that involves the dog chasing the child, nipping or jumping up.

Bear hugs

The muzzle and scruff of a dog's neck are very sensitive. When the dog was a puppy, this is where its mother would hold it to assert her authority, and when dogs fight attention is focused on the head. If a child grabs a dog around the head or envelops its neck in a bear hug it could be perceived as threatening, and the dog may react aggressively. Encourage your children to pet the dog gently on its back. This will subtly reinforce the child's dominant position in the family hierarchy.

Quietly does it

When children are excited, their voices become high-pitched and their body movements are often erratic. If they are holding their arms up, a dog may see it as an invitation to jump up. Training a dog to lie down or sit on command is important to prevent this.

Children sometimes repeat a dog's name so often that the dog "tunes out" completely and ignores them. Encourage your children to say the dog's name once and reward it with a treat or a toy as soon as it pays attention to them.

What's in a name?

The children will want to be involved in choosing a name for your dog. Bear in mind that the best names are short, with one or two syllables, and that it must be easy to say and shout. Remember, too, that at many vet offices your dog's name will be tagged onto your surname, so if you think it might be embarrassing to have the nurse shout out something like 'Cutie Pie Jones' or 'Sneezy Smith' in the middle of a busy waiting room, it might be time for a rethink.

Signing up for
puppy school

Involve the entire family in your dog's training program. It is important that the dog behaves well for every family member and that everyone knows the commands and signals that are being used. Everyone in the family should also be aware of the different objects, people and situations to which the puppy has been exposed to in its socialization program (see pages 48–49).

Training tips

The basics that your dog will need to learn to keep it safe and able to enjoy family life are:

Heeling on and off the leash
Recall
Sit
Stay
Wait
Down

Some dogs take longer to train than others, so encourage everyone in the family to be patient and to follow the philosophy that "practice makes perfect". Getting the puppy used to hearing its name, coming when it is called, accepting treats from different people, being handled regularly and having its collar put on and taken off are all things that can be learned from day one.

Making time for several short training sessions throughout the day will be far more beneficial than one long session, which may physically or mentally tire the dog.

Heel, boy!

Training your dog to be obedient and walk to heel calmly, both on and off the leash, without pulling is very important. Large dogs will simply drag or pull children over if they are not trained properly. Choose a collar and leash that are suitable for the breed and type of dog you have. A strong, short leash will give whoever is handling the dog more control than a long flexi-lead.

Make leash training sessions short — no more than five minutes at first. If you have space, start the sessions indoors. Gradually extend the length of time the puppy goes on the leash and take it out into the yard to try walking where there is distraction. Your puppy will probably find right-hand turns easiest in the beginning, so concentrate on these until it is confident enough to negotiate a left turn.

It's a good idea to buy several waist bags so that every family member can wear one when training the dog. Fill the bags with treats so that you always have some handy, ready to reward the dog when it has worked well.

Obedience classes

Once your dog has graduated from its puppy socialization classes, sign up for some obedience training. Personal recommendation from other dog owners are often a good starting point for finding a reputable trainer. Alternatively, your vet may be able to recommend someone or there may be notices up at the office.

Take your family along and observe a few classes before you commit to signing up for training. Are there other children in the class? Do people feel free to ask questions and are they answered fully?

Child's-eye view

"My auntie's dog is really cool. She can balance a biscuit on her nose and when you tell her to she throws it in the air and catches it. That's the best trick ever." Maddie, age 7

Tip to parents

Once your dog has mastered the basics of obedience you can have lots of fun teaching it tricks. Dogs enjoy the mental and physical stimulation of learning, and the whole family will enjoy showing off its party tricks.

Walking the dog

1 Begin in a quiet room where there are no distractions. The child might find it convenient to keep a handful of dog treats in a waist bag, for easy access. Ask her to put the collar and leash on the puppy and to speak in a calm, reassuring way.

2 The puppy should be on the child's left side, while she holds the end of the leash in her right hand and the rest of the leash in her left hand, closer to the puppy's head.

3 The child should walk up and down the room in a straight line, saying the word "heel" as she does so and offering the puppy lots of verbal encouragement as it walks beside her.

4 Finish the session with a treat and enthusiastic stroking.

Clicker training
and beyond

When your dog has learned the basics, you and your children may find that you enjoy training so much you want to take things further, perhaps even working toward competitions. You can buy books and DVDs on dog training or you can attend classes where techniques are taught. The advantage of classes is that you and your dog are able to socialize and have fun with like-minded people.

Training is fun

Let your child get involved with as much of the puppy's training as possible. You can teach her the basic training skills, then let her take over. Encourage her to always reward the dog's good behavior, to be patient and to say the dog's name whenever it is walking towards her. Dissuade her from using words that may confuse the dog, expecting it to do complicated tricks early in training or being negative toward the dog if it fails to understand. Training sessions should be kept short to avoid tiring out the dog.

Click it!

Clickers encourage the dog to work out for itself what you want it to do – a process that helps engrain behavior into its memory. A clicker is used to teach a dog that it has done something well and is being rewarded for it. When the dog does something you want it to do, such as coming when it is called, you click to "mark" the behavior and then give the dog a reward. It

Clicker training

1 Your child should have some treats ready and stand near the dog (or kneel down, if the dog is small). Let the child give it a few treats to get its interest.

2 Encourage the child to offer a treat and to click when the dog looks at her to see if she is going to offer another.

will soon realize that every time it hears a click it has done something you like and will associate it with getting a reward. When this happens it will always come to you when it is called because it hopes to get another reward, whether or not it gets a click for it.

Explain to your children that it's a bit like when they do something good at school and are rewarded with a star, or do a good job of tidying up their bedrooms and get a special treat from mom and dad. Every time they tidy their room they are hoping that they will be praised and might even get a little treat, but if they don't always get a reward they might try a little harder and even clean another room as well in the hope of getting a better treat. Dogs are just the same.

Take it further

Children will enjoy showing off their dog's skills to their friends and family and may want to teach the dog tricks, such as nosing a ball around the yard, playing follow the leader, jumping through a

hoop and walking tall on its back legs. All of these are simply extensions of the basic training the dog learns in the very beginning.

Contact your national kennel club for details of activities for young handlers. It may be possible to attend a summer camp or training days, where youngsters are given the opportunity to camp out with their dogs and try a variety of different sports and activities, such as flyball, agility and heelwork to music. These events are fun, and it is wonderful how confident it makes the children and the dogs as they blossom under the tutelage of experienced kennel club members.

3 The child should throw a treat out in front, clicking just before the dog eats it. Repeat this training several times. The technique can be used for teaching the dog anything, but only click once for each stage, even if you offer more than one treat.

Clicker training

You can incorporate a clicker into all the training routines in this book. Once you and your dog have gotten used to it, clicking gets progressively easier.

ENCOURAGE your dog so that it performs the DESIRED BEHAVIOR.

CLICK! TREAT

PRACTICE until your dog can easily do the moves following your signals.

Once your dog understands the action, give it a VERBAL COMMAND.

CLICK! TREAT

PRACTICE so that your dog performs the action simply on voice commands.

Add a refined visual signal if desired.

Won't he
come
back?

It can be really frustrating when your dog won't come back because it has found something more interesting to investigate. Training your puppy to come when called is one of the most important lessons you and your children can teach. It will allow you to walk your dog off leash with confidence, letting it explore and meet people and other dogs on its own.

More clicker training

1 The child should stand a little way from the dog, then call the dog's name once and rattle the treat container.

2 The child should click as soon as the dog turns to look at her, marking the fact that it has given her its attention on hearing its name.

3 When the dog walks back to the child, she should offer a treat. Ask everyone in the family to try the exercise, repeating it several times a day and being generous with praise and treats. The dog will then make the connection between coming when called and earning a treat.

Here, boy!

If the whole family is out for walk and the dog refuses to return when it is called, the children might run after the dog to try to catch it. However, your dog is quite likely to interpret this as a great game of chase or hide-and-seek and will probably run even faster with the child in hot pursuit. Your child might have more success if she calls the dog's name to get its attention and then hides from him, which could arouse its curiosity sufficiently to get it to come back and look for her. Of course, this should be done only if it is safe — that is, if there is no traffic around — and

remember that dogs should not be encouraged to chase after children.

If you know you are going somewhere with lots of distractions, get your child to take along a supply of high-value treats or toys. She can use these to keep the dog's attention. A boring, dry biscuit may be insufficient to tempt a dog, but if it knows she is carrying diced chicken or cooked liver it may respond more promptly. If your dog is more motivated by toys and games, rather than by edible treats, keep a highly prized toy for it to play with only when it returns after a period off the leash.

3

Question time

Q *I've tried everything. Why won't my dog come back when I call him?*

If you or someone else has ever used any kind of physical punishment on the dog when it has returned to you this will make it even less inclined to return the next time it is tempted to run off. Why should it go back to someone who is going to hit it? The dog will quickly begin to develop negative associations and feel nervous about returning to you. Whenever any aspect of your dog's training breaks down, take it back a stage and retrain using the techniques you have learned. The more you train your dog, the more likely it is that it will come back when you call it.

A The dog needs to view coming back to you as a worthwhile experience and a time when it will get a reward, whether that is food, toys, praise or a game. One of the main reasons a dog does not want to return is because it views coming back as the end of its freedom and fun. Practice getting the dog to come to you for a reward and then allowing it to run off and play again, to help it realize that this is not the case.

Sitting pretty
and waiting

Teaching a dog to sit on command is an easy training exercise, and also a very useful one. The command is a convenient way of calming an excitable dog, particularly if it is involved in behavior such as play-biting or jumping up at people — a large dog can easily knock a small child off his feet. Simply being able to tell the dog to sit will immediately diffuse the situation.

Sit!

Your child can easily teach this command (see right), but supervise him at first. Dogs tend naturally to drop into a sit when they are anticipating something good, such as the arrival of food or a favorite person. The child will need a leash, clicker, some tasty treats and a quiet room to practice in.

Wait!

Once the dog understands the "sit" command, your child can take things a stage further by waiting a couple of seconds until he clicks and rewards. This should be repeated several times, gradually increasing the wait to five or six seconds and introducing the "wait" command. The child should then take one or two steps back. If the dog remains sitting, he should click and return to give it a treat.

He should repeat the maneuver several times, walking slightly further back each time and always clicking at the furthest point away before returning and offering the treat. It is useful to teach the dog a release expression, such as "OK", so that it knows the wait is over.

Jumping up

Be consistent and never allow your dog to jump at anyone. Encourage whoever you meet to ignore the dog until it sits. This means avoiding eye contact, folding their arms and showing total disinterest. As soon as the dog goes into a sit, it can be rewarded with a treat and praise. If the behavior is very bad, you can try interrupting the dog's actions with a noise distraction, such as a plastic bottle filled with small stones, which you can rattle loudly whenever it jumps up.

Teaching your dog to sit

1 Your child should put on the dog's leash and say its name, giving it a treat when it looks at him. Encourage the child to hold another treat in the underhand position so that the dog can sniff it but not snatch it from his hand.

2 With the dog in front of him, the child should turn over his hand so that the treat is in the overhand position. He should position his hand above the dog's nose and move it slightly back, in the direction of its tail. This will make the dog's head tilt up and its back end drop down.

3 The moment the dog drops into a sit, the child should click and offer the treat. Repeat this training several times, gradually building in the verbal command "sit" and eventually dispensing with the clicks and treats.

Will he
stay?

"Stay" differs from the "wait" command. Your child is not simply asking the dog to be patient and override its instincts to do something, such as eat, go through a door or pick up a ball. Teaching the "stay" command means that your child will be able to walk away, talk to a friend, move into another room or go into a store and trust the dog to stay in the same place until she returns.

Staying still

1 The child should put the dog into a sit position (see pages 80–81) and then gradually build the time the dog remains in position, praising it and offering treats over an extended period.

2 The child can begin to move away from the dog, either walking backward or moving to the side. She should give the verbal command "stay" and hold the palm of her hand out as a visual symbol for the dog to remain in place.

Stay!

"Stay" is a key command if your child wants to participate in obedience training, because during a competition the dog will be expected to stay in one place for three or four minutes, oblivious to any distractions. In competitions, the dog may also be asked to obey the "stay" command from different positions — sit, down or stand.

When the dog obeys your child's "stay" command, it is an expression of the confidence between child and dog, showing that the dog is willing to listen to your child and trusts her enough to remain on its own until she comes back. Obedience is achieved by teaching slowly, with great patience, always aiming to release the dog just before it moves. Your child can start to teach "stay" when the dog is capable of sitting still beside her for 30–40 seconds.

Once the basic command has been mastered, the child can gradually increase the time or distance that she moves away from the dog. On each occasion, she should return, reward and give the release command (such as "OK", see page 80). Eventually, she can take it to the next stage by returning to the dog without giving the release command and moving away again.

3 After a second or two the child can use the clicker once and move back toward the dog, offering lots of praise and a treat or toy as a reward. A release command will help the dog to realize that it is now free to move. If the dog breaks position, the child should simply put it back into a sit and give the "sit" and "stay" commands again, returning more quickly so it begins to understand that it is being rewarded for not moving. Time and distance away from the dog should then be gradually increased.

Do! encourage your child to …

Teach the "stay" command only when the dog has learned to sit without rewards
Train in a quiet place, with no distractions
Gradually introduce distractions, such as children and other dogs, once the dog understands the "stay" command
Slowly build up the time your dog stays

Don't! encourage your child to …

Rush the training process and progress too quickly
Get frustrated if your dog keeps breaking the stay
Train for extended periods so the dog gets bored
Test the dog by leaving it for too long

Child's-eye view

"I'd like it if my dog stayed outside my classroom when I was at school. But I guess that would be way too long a stay." Matthew, age 9

Tip to parents

Don't set a young dog up to fail by asking it to remain in a stay for too long. If it breaks the stay, never scold, simply put it back into position and try again. Always end sessions on a good note.

When a dog is
down at heel

If any of your children's friends are nervous of dogs, they will find it reassuring to see that the dog is trained and can be relied upon to drop into a down position when asked. For dogs to do this they must have developed a bond with their handler, because this is a vulnerable, submissive position for them and an indication that they respect the handler's role as leader of the pack.

Tip to parents
Ask children to use the word "down" only when they want the dog to drop into a down position. Using the word in other contexts, such as to get out of the car or off a chair, will confuse the dog.

Getting the dog to lie down

1 With the dog in a standing position, the child should hold out a treat in the underhand position and call the dog. The dog should be allowed to sniff the treat, but not take it.

2 As the child moves the treat hand slightly behind the dog's head, the dog will drop into a sitting position.

Down!

Some breeds, such as the Border Collie, drop into a down very readily, but others, particularly large breeds, such as the Great Dane, find it more difficult to coordinate themselves quickly. A thin-skinned dog, such as a Greyhound will not appreciate being asked to lie down on a cold, damp, concrete floor. Older dogs, or dogs suffering from arthritis or some other types of joint problems, will struggle to get up and down, so use this command with care.

The training can be developed further by teaching the dog to stand up again as soon as the "stand" command is given. The child should stand in front of the dog and put it into a sit position, then hold out the treat hand toward the dog's nose level so that it can sniff it. The child can then pull his hand back very slightly to lure the dog toward him. As soon as the dog stands, the child should click and give the treat. The training should be repeated several times, gradually building in the word "stand", and then tried again when the dog is in a down position.

Motivation

As the dog learns a command, food treats should be gradually withdrawn. Rewarding every second or third time, instead of every time, will help to motivate the dog to repeat the command. This is also how many types of bad behaviors are unwittingly encouraged. For example, if a dog begs when its family is eating a meal and occasionally someone gives in, it will continue to beg because it will always be hoping for that one time when its begging is rewarded. If it is never fed at the table it will not beg.

3 The child should then lure the dog from a sit into a down, moving the treat hand slightly forward and down. The dog's front legs will move out until it cannot go any further without dropping into a down position. As soon as he does this, the child should click and offer the treat. He should repeat this exercise several times, saying the word "down" as the dog drops. As the dog begins to understand the association of dropping into a down with getting a reward, it will do so on the verbal command only.

Roll over
and die

Children are delighted when their dog is able to do one or two tricks, and the roll over is a relatively easy one to teach once your dog understands the "down" command. A roll over involves the dog dropping into the down position, rolling right over onto its back and jumping back up again afterward. It looks very impressive and some dogs, particularly small ones, seem to enjoy doing it.

Offering a bait

The trick is taught through luring, so your child will need a clicker and a supply of selected high-value treats (such as small chicken pieces) that the dog will enjoy working for. A roll over is actually a sequence of separate moves and it is taught gradually. Encourage your child to teach each part separately until the dog begins to understand what he wants it to do.

Dead cool

Once your dog has learned the roll over, your child can get it to play dead by using the "wait" command to stop the move halfway through. He

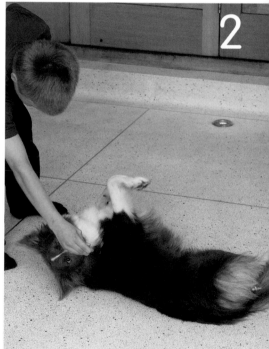

Roll over!

1 The child should ask the dog to drop into a down position (see pages 84–85) and allow the dog to sniff the treat.

2 Encourage the child to move the treat hand toward the dog's shoulder. He will need to arch his arm over the dog's head, letting the dog sniff the treat. He should do this slowly and steadily, until the dog becomes unbalanced. At this point the dog will flop onto its side, and the child should click and offer a reward.

should click and treat at this point, and practice several times using the verbal command "dead". When the dog understands the "dead" command, it will drop instantly to the floor, as if its been shot, which can look very dramatic!

Safety first

If your child wants to teach the dog to do tricks, you should always take into account the dog's age, health and disposition. Bear in mind that, as dogs grow older, it may become more difficult for them to perform the tricks they did easily when they were younger.

Do! encourage your child to …

Teach this trick slowly, clicking and treating for each section of the move before asking for it in one smooth movement

Build in a verbal command, such as "roll over"

Give the dog enough time to digest its last meal before practicing this trick

Don't! encourage your child to …

Overuse the commands because your dog will tire of doing them

Allow frustration to develop if the dog doesn't want to perform; go back to something fun that he likes doing and try again later

3 While the dog is still lying on its side the child should get another treat and continue to lure it over. Its head will follow the direction of the child's hand and its legs will follow as it rolls over onto the right side. The child should click during this roll over movement and, when the dog has flopped onto its side, give the treat.

4 Finally, the child should take another treat and lure the dog from its side into an ordinary down position. To do this he will need to hold the treat out toward the dog's nose and move it slowly toward its feet. He should click and offer the treat when the dog has returned to its starting position.

Paws
for thought

Sit up and beg, shake paws and high-five are great tricks that will delight your children and boost their street-cred. Dogs must learn to balance to do these tricks, so warn children not to be too enthusiastic or they will push the dog over and make it lose confidence. As with all training, involve your children if they are old enough but also supervise them, especially in the early stages.

Sit up and beg

1 Your child should begin by teaching the dog to sit up and beg. She should put the dog in a sit and stand or kneel in front of it, holding a treat out toward its nose.

2 The child should move her hand up and back slightly so that the dog tilts its head backward and lifts its front paws off the ground. As soon as both paws come off the ground, she should click and reward.

3 She should repeat the procedure several times, each time asking the dog to lift its paws a little higher until it eventually finds its point of balance. She can begin to withhold the click and treat for a second or two to encourage the dog to remain up on its haunches. A verbal command, such as "beg", or "say please", can be built in to trigger the move.

Shake on it

Your child should put the dog into a sit and kneel in front of her, holding a treat in her hand so the dog can smell it. She should move her hand slightly so it shifts its weight from the paw she wants it to lift. Most dogs will lift a paw to try to get the treat and, if it does, she should click and treat. If the dog seems reluctant, she can pick up its paw, click and treat.

Ask her to keep practicing, adding a verbal command just before she clicks and using separate words for each front paw, such as "paw" for the right and "pat" for the left. She can develop the trick by holding a treat in one hand and opening out her other hand next to the paw she wants the dog to lift, clicking and treating as soon as it does so. Eventually the dog will learn that it gets a reward for lifting its paw when it sees the child's open hand.

High-five

This trick is basically the same as giving a paw, but instead of holding her palm out your child should turn her hand over in a high-five. Click and treat as soon as the dog makes contact, building in the command "high-five". With practice the dog should be able to do a nice pat-a-cake rhythm using both paws. As a variation, your child can put the dog into a beg and hold both her hands out in a high-five, clicking as the dog touches both hands at the same time and then rewarding.

ABOVE: Your child will impress her friends to no end if she can shake paws and do a high-five with her dog!

Do! encourage your child to …

Take her time and practice these moves so that the dog will eventually respond to visual cues

Kneel down if necessary and get close enough to the dog to make it easy for it to make contact with her hands

Don't! encourage your child to …

Try sit up and beg or a high-five before the dog is six months old or its developing joints could be damaged

Ask older dogs with joint problems to do upright tricks

Expect young dogs or large breeds to be able to balance immediately; it may be necessary to hold a paw to steady the dog at first

Fun and games
for all the family

The more games your children can think of to play with the dog, the more it will enjoy life and respond to people. Here are just a few ideas to get the whole family started. To stop the dog losing interest, encourage the children to allow the dog to win sometimes. However, don't let it win too often or it will start to think that it has moved a few rungs up the family hierarchy.

Treasure hunt

Ask your children to lay a trail of treats for the dog around the house and yard. Hold its collar and let it watch before releasing it and telling the dog to find the treats. Dogs enjoy these kinds of games and can search out treats hidden in quite difficult places, such as under upturned plant pots. Some dogs, such as Beagles, will be better than others, but if you can find something exciting for them to search for, such as a delicious food treat or a special toy, most dogs will join in the game.

Bubble trouble

Believe it or not, you can now buy pots of chicken- and bacon-scented bubbles specially for dogs. Your children will have great fun blowing bubble trails for the dog to try to catch. It will be amusing to watch its face as it snaps at a bubble and it disappears before its eyes.

Activity toys

Pet stores and supermarkets often stock strong, rubber, bouncy toys, to be filled with delicious treats. The treats are dispensed only when the dog rolls the toy or moves it around. You can either use dried dog treats, large enough not to drop out easily, or buy tubes of meat-flavored filling, which can be squirted into the toy.

You can also buy rubber toys with ropes attached that make them easier to throw, or find activity balls, which are filled with treats and left with the dog to play with. These will help to keep your dog entertained if you have to leave for an hour or two.

Hide and seek

Hold your dog by the collar and ask the children to run and hide. When they are out of sight, release the dog and ask it to find them. Your children can reward the dog with treats when it manages to find them.

Buried treasure

If your dog likes to dig, allocate a special spot in the yard and bury a few treats or rawhide chews just below the surface so that it can enjoy digging and looking for them.

Doggy paddle

Dogs with thin skins and some older dogs do not enjoy water, and if your dog is not willing don't try to force it to participate. Some breeds, such as Labradors, are very fond of swimming and will jump into the nearest river at any opportunity, so check the water is safe beforehand. Your children will have fun throwing a ball or toy into the water for it, but avoid sticks, which can splinter in the dog's throat. Swimming is a tiring activity and so don't allow your dog to overexert itself.

Musical chairs

Play some music for your children and ask one of them to tell the dog to drop into the down position when it stops. As soon as the dog drops down, they can all run to find a chair. If the dog breaks position before the music starts again they will have to get off and put the dog back into a down. Remove a chair for each round of the game.

ABOVE: A Kong is a favorite toy for dogs. It can be filled with treats and then hidden for the dog to hunt down.

OPPOSITE LEFT: Your child can lay a treasure trail of treats, to see if the dog will manage to find every one.

OPPOSITE RIGHT: Watch the puppy go wild as it chases after the chicken-flavored bubbles!

Question time

Q *Is it okay for my child to play tug-of-war with the dog?*

A Some trainers do not advocate this type of play, particularly with children, as dogs may get overexcited and knock over the child. And it is not a desirable game for retriever-type dogs as it tends to encourage a hard mouth. However, if you have sufficient control over the dog to stop the game on command, there is no reason you can't do this. Avoid playing tug-of-war with old clothing, because the dog will not be able to differentiate between these clothes and those you don't want it to have.

Agility training
and flyball

If you think your children would enjoy combining obedience training with speed, then they could well enjoy agility work. Agility exercises test the dog's fitness and aptitude, as well as the handler's ability to control it as it runs and jumps over and through a variety of obstacles. Intelligent, active breeds such as Border Collies have a particular talent for this sort of work.

Jump to it

To find out more about agility, contact your national kennel club for details of local shows. If your children would like to try the sport, check for junior training days or special classes in which they can enroll. Dogs should be over 12 months when they start agility training and at least 18 months before competing.

There are a number of maximum jump heights, according to the size of the dog, but each organization has its own height classes and rules, so ensure you know what these are before competing. The jumps are all lightweight and knock down easily to reduce the risk of injury. Dogs tackle a course of up to 20 obstacles and incur penalties for missing one, knocking one down or failing to touch a "contact" point. Each round is timed against the clock, and there is a maximum time so that handlers don't take the easy way out and just wander around. This sport is physically challenging, and your dog must be fit enough to participate, so make an appointment with your vet to weigh your dog and give it a checkup before you start training.

Even if you don't want to compete at shows your children will enjoy setting up an obstacle course at home to see if their dog is likely to enjoy this kind of work. Obstacles to try include:

Collapsible tunnels
Hoops
Tires
Weave poles
See-saw
Jumps (must knock down easily)
Long jump

In competitions the dogs are expected to cross an A-ramp, but don't ask your dog to attempt

Approximate jump sizes

Dog size	Dog measurement	Jump size
Small	Less than 14 inches (35 cm) at the withers	10–14 inches (25–35 cm)
Medium	Over 14 inches (35 cm), but under 17 inches (43 cm) at the withers	14–18 inches (35–45 cm)
Large	Over 17 inches (43 cm) at the withers	22–26 inches (55–65 cm)

this unless you have been trained to do so by a professional agility instructor. Once you have set up a mini-obstacle course at home, your children will enjoy trying to negotiate it. You can time the course or set up two identical courses so that any of your children's friends with dogs can race against each other. Don't forget to give your child a waist bag full of treats to reward the dog and to help lure it over obstacles.

Flyball

If your dog is fit and healthy and enjoys energetic games, you might want to try this fast new dog sport, which many children love. It is a race between two teams of four dogs, which run down a line of small hurdles as fast as they can until they reach a box containing tennis balls. When a dog reaches the box he has to trigger it with his paws so that a tennis ball springs out and he can catch it in his mouth and race back to the start, ready for the next dog to set off. There is,

of course, lots of verbal encouragement from both the teams and the spectators. Dogs that compete accumulate points and will eventually earn medals, certificates and other awards.

Flyball is a highly energetic sport, and the dogs find it exciting, so a basic level of obedience is necessary. The dog must be very well socialized and able to cope with the distractions of having lots of other dogs around.

BELOW: A collapsible tunnel does not take up much storage space, but will give your dog endless fun!

OPPOSITE: Hold the hoop while your child uses a treat to tempt the dog to jump through.

> ## Tip to parents
> Don't allow children to take their dog around obstacle courses unsupervised. Children don't have the necessary experience to judge the consequences of an activity and may inadvertently ask the dog to do something that is potentially dangerous for it.

Let's have a canine carnival!

There is nothing that children like more than a good party, so combining one for them and their dogs is sure to be a success. You don't need a special occasion, any day will do — it could be your dog's birthday or the anniversary of when you got it. Provide plenty of dog-friendly foods so that children are not tempted to share their sandwiches and chips with their canine companions.

Any excuse for a party

If you plan a summer party you can have an outdoor venue, perhaps in your garden or a local park. Some beaches are dog-friendly and would be a perfect place to hold a summer picnic or barbecue. In the winter you could rent a hall, such as the one where your dog-training classes are usually held, but check that this is acceptable with the owners beforehand.

Choose a selection of dogs you know get along well with each other and ask their owners to confirm that they are coming so you can cater for everyone. Children will enjoy being involved in making up a guest list and creating special invitations to send to the dogs. Put a note on the invitation saying that you look forward to some doggy entertainment, if any of the dogs have a particular party trick they would like to practice before the big day. This could well motivate the human guests into teaching their dogs a trick or two that they can show off.

Fancy dress parties are also always fun. Each child and their dog should dress up as a team,

such as Batman and Robin or a king and queen. You can award a prize for the best outfits.

How long?

A couple of hours will probably be the maximum amount of time you need for the party. Prepare a timetable so that you know what is going to happen and when. You could begin with a group walk so that everyone gets to know each other and the dogs can relax in each other's company. When you return it is an ideal time to put the food out and enjoy spending time together. Don't forget to put out plenty of water bowls, too.

Doggy games

If lots of children are coming, you can plan some games that they can play while the dogs digest their food. Choose dog-themed games, such as pinning the ID tag on the dog's collar or musical kennels, using hoops or mats. Afterward you could ask if any owners have dogs that have learned tricks they would like to perform. This

should lead to loud applause, even if the tricks go wrong. You can also award a prize to each performer, such as a certificate or a rosette.

Finish with some games that people and dogs can enjoy together, such as a treat and spoon race (rewarding the dogs with the treats at the end). If you've had time to set it up beforehand, an obstacle race will make a good final game (and see pages 90–93 for more game ideas).

Give your canine guests a bag of dog goodies as they leave. It's sensible to prepare and label them beforehand, so they are easy to hand out. You could include some homemade treats, a ball or a small toy — and don't forget a little something for the host dog.

ABOVE: Puppies love playing with balloons, wrapping paper and presents — so watch what goes on the floor.

OPPOSITE: Fancy dress will make the party an extra-special occasion for the human guests.

Dancing with dogs

Most children love to sing, dance and generally have fun with music, and heelwork to music, or freestyle heeling, is a great way of combining all of these things, as well as involving the family dog. It is also an enjoyable way of continuing the dog's training and making sure that it remains physically and mentally stimulated, which is particularly important for very active, intelligent breeds.

ABOVE: Mary Ray, a leading heelwork to music trainer, has developed a strong bond with her canine troupe.

OPPOSITE: Your child will have great fun dressing up and creating her own heelwork to music routine.

What's involved?

Heelwork to music (HTM), also known as freestyle heeling can be performed at any level by adults and children, whether done competitively or simply to entertain. In a heelwork to music routine, at least half the moves should be with the dog in a heel position, keeping its shoulder level with the handler's knee while the handler moves to music. This could mean marching together, for example, or doing figure-eights. In a freestyle routine, the dog can perform a greater variety of moves, such as twists or jumps, anywhere in the arena.

Dressing up

Children love to dress up, and heelwork to music provides plenty of opportunities for fancy outfits. However, if they want to dress up their canine partner, they should be gently reminded that heelwork is a sport rather than some kind of circus act. In competitions, dogs are allowed to wear only a bandanna or collar. Props are allowed though, as long as they are part of the routine, so if your dog is happy to carry a shopping basket or a magic wand in its mouth you can really show off its skills.

Music maestro

You can use any type of music in HTM, with or without words. Young children can even make up a dance routine to a nursery rhyme if they want to. Having a music system is just about all you need, as long as someone is ready to press the start and stop buttons when needed.

Find out more

Heelwork to music is a great spectator sport that expresses the bond between dog and owner and combines the skill of the handler with the beauty and versatility of the dog. Your local dog-training club may have details of classes or shows where you and your child can see HTM in action. Alternatively, contact your national kennel club to find out more. They may offer training days, when junior handlers will have the opportunity to try out the sport. If your child is interested in competing, the dog must be registered at the national kennel club.

You can also buy books and DVDs on the subject, and an Internet search will provide you with contact details and information about the clubs dedicated to the sport.

Question time

Q We've got a German Shepherd that is quite well trained, but will it be too big and clumsy to do heelwork to music?

A Any breed and height of dog can try heelwork to music, provided they are fit and healthy enough. The beauty of this sport is that you can create your own routine, which should last for up to four minutes, and choose music and moves that will show off your dog's physique and personality. Many German Shepherds compete in HTM at upper levels, but, as with any dog, if your dog is older or suffers from back or joint problems you should avoid moves, such as walking on the hind legs, that are likely to exacerbate them. The activity is a great way of channeling the dog's energy.

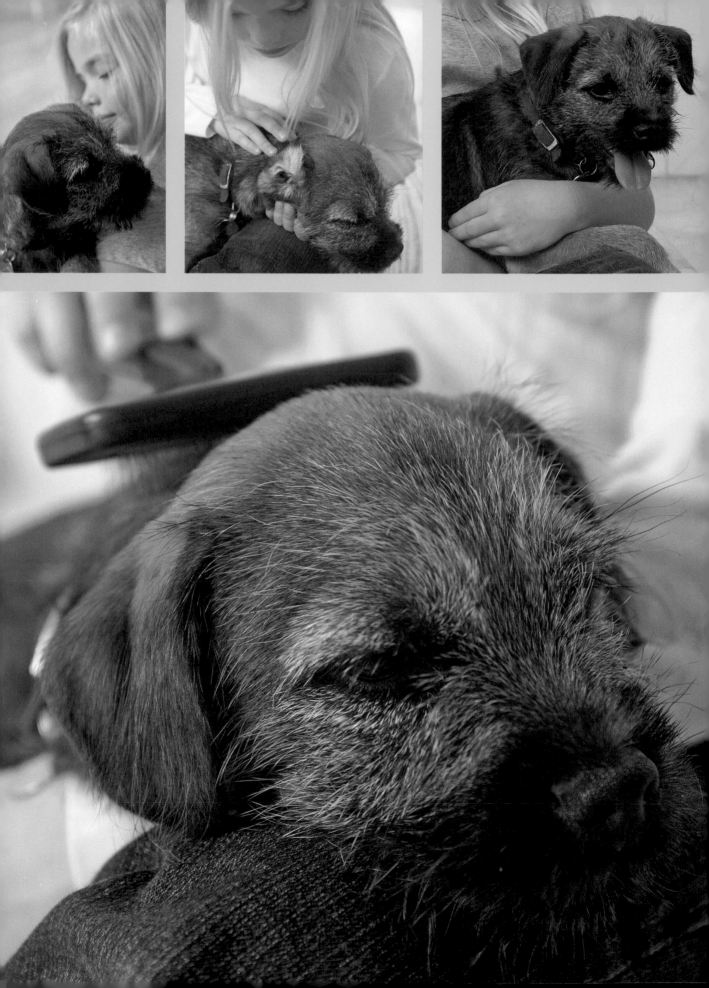

chapter 7

Health and safety

This chapter looks at basic hygiene and safety rules, from getting rid of fleas to protecting your dog outside the home. Some diseases can be passed on to children by dogs, so it is important to make children aware that they must wash their hands after touching a dog, particularly before meals. Small children often think that turning the tap on and off constitutes hand washing, so supervise them to make sure they use soap and water thoroughly.

Deworming

The most common parasitic worms in dogs are roundworms and tapeworms. A puppy that is infested with roundworms looks sickly and has a pot-belly. The roundworms are sometimes vomited and resemble pale, curled elastic bands. There are two types, *Toxocara canis* and *Toxascaris leonine*, but only the worms of *T. canis* can be passed to humans. Although it is rare, the eggs can survive in soil for up to four years, so keeping your garden cleared of dog feces is important.

The eggs of tapeworms resemble grains of rice, and if your dog is infested they may be visible around the anus. The tapeworm attaches itself to the wall of the dog's intestines, and the eggs are excreted in feces.

Don't forget that telling children they could catch worms from the dog will probably make them think of earthworms! Explain that these are special worms, called parasites, that live inside the dog. Although it is quite rare for children to become infested by the family pet, a child may come into contact with the parasite in playgrounds or parks where dog fouling has occurred and the feces have not been removed.

Worm eggs can cause toxicariasis (sometimes called toxocara), which can cause allergic reactions and even blindness. Some worms cause hydatid disease, which affects the liver, lungs and brain, although this is more prevalent in sheep-farming areas. Toxicariasis is extremely dangerous to pregnant women because it can cause major damage to, or even the death of, the fetus. Heartworms, causing serious illness, are spread by mosquitoes.

Thankfully, deworming products obtained from your vet are extremely effective at killing worms. These are given orally or as local treatments, when a tiny amount is squirted onto the dog's neck. A puppy should have been dewormed when it was two or three weeks old to kill any parasites that were passed to it in its mother's milk. Deworm your child's dog regularly – usually three or four times a year. Deworming treatments will protect the dog when it comes into contact with other dogs and prevent the transmission of parasites.

Vaccinate
and stay safe

Just as you protect children against diseases by making sure that they have all the necessary immunizations, you should also protect your child's dog from potentially life-threatening diseases. If you are planning to travel with your dog or board it in a kennel while you are on vacation, you will have to provide records to show that all its vaccinations are up to date.

Defleaing your dog

1 Ask your child to stand the dog on a white towel, which will show evidence of fleas that drop out as she combs the dog. If you have a light-colored dog you might be able to see fleas easily, but it is more difficult with darker haired dogs and a close-pronged flea comb is useful.

2 Your child should begin at the head and comb carefully toward the back, paying special attention to the ears, collar area, base of the tail and between the toes.

Common diseases

Most vets recommend that dogs are given core vaccines against the following diseases: distemper virus, adenoviral hepatitis, canine parvovirus and leptospirosis. The latter is common in rats and transmissible to humans. Dogs that swim in rivers are at risk, and the disease causes jaundice and liver failure.

Non-core vaccines are also available, including those against canine parainfluenza and *Bordetella bronchiseptica*. These are both agents associated with kennel cough and are usually needed if a dog goes into a kennel or is to be shown.

Your vet will advise you on the frequency of booster shots, which may be required annually or every two to three years. Also, regular, preventative treatment of heartworms is necessary in many areas of North America.

Fleas and ticks

Safeguarding your dog and your home against fleas and ticks is another way to protect against disease and expensive vet bills. Unfortunately, because most houses have central heating, fleas can thrive all year round.

Many complementary therapies can repel fleas but not actually kill them, and the most effective preparations for killing fleas and ticks are available from your vet. Prescribed treatments take the form of shampoos, tablets, sprays or local treatments. These are effective, but they contain chemicals, so dispose of all packaging carefully, away from young children.

If your child's dog scratches itself frequently, it could have fleas. Fleas can hop between dogs and cats, but they can't live on humans. However, they can bite and some people are allergic to this. Ticks are small, gray, pea-sized creatures that anchor onto the skin with their mouths, feeding on blood. They can spread several diseases including Lyme disease. If you pull them off, don't leave any part of the tick embedded in the skin. Fortunately, most anti-flea preparations are also designed to kill ticks.

3 If any evidence of fleas or eggs is discovered during the check, a flea treatment obtained from your vet should be applied. Wash hands thoroughly afterward and dispose of the packaging carefully.

Question time

Q *Is it true that fleas can live in the furniture? Always treat your home, other pets and bedding with a proprietary flea treatment. Your vet can advise you on the best product to use. Vacuuming your home thoroughly and steam cleaning will also help control the problem.*

A Fleas can live quite happily in carpets and soft furnishings for up to two years. They stay there dormant (which means asleep), waiting for someone's dog or cat to walk past so they can leap on and take up residence. In two days a female flea will start laying up to 50 eggs a day. So you see that it's important we check your dog regularly!

Traffic safety
on the roads

If you have socialized your child's dog thoroughly, particularly during the first few months of his life, it should already have been exposed to different levels of traffic and learned not to react to it. Seeing-eye and hearing dogs are so used to traffic that they can guide their humans through the busiest of streets without flinching, but this is achieved only after extended, dedicated training.

Walking in the street

1 Find a quiet place where you can sit some distance away from traffic. Get the child and dog to sit quietly together, so that the dog becomes used to hearing the noise of traffic and to seeing cars that are not moving very fast. Ask your child to reassure the dog verbally and to reward it with a treat when it sits quietly and focuses its attention on the child.

2 When the dog can sit quietly, the child should stand up and walk the dog toward traffic and back again. Tell your child to remember to offer a reward every time the dog walks calmly or looks at her, but to try to ignore any negative behavior.

Traffic calming

Taking time to train the dog to walk calmly on the leash is particularly important when you have children, because larger dogs can be strong enough to pull a child into oncoming traffic. If you sense that your dog is nervous in traffic, try to find a special toy and use it as a distraction. Choose something that you can carry in your pocket or hide in a waist bag and take it with you when you are walking the dog. When you are not out on walks, allow the dog limited access to this toy. This will help to maintain its importance, which will mean that the dog's interest is in it when you do produce it, and it will help to override other instincts, such as fear of the traffic.

Make sure you always put the dog on a strong leash, and hold it carefully in two hands. If you have a strong dog do not wrap the leash around your hand or you could be dragged. If you need more control, try fitting a harness or head collar on the dog. For safety reasons never allow children to walk nervous dogs in traffic.

Slowly does it

Take each stage slowly. If there is no improvement, enlist the help of a professional pet behaviorist, who will draw up a behavior modification program specifically for your dog. A pet behaviorist will also be able to give you advice on how to stop the dog from chasing cars or cyclists, perhaps by using noise distractions, such as a plastic bottle filled with pebbles, or special dog training disks.

Always be especially careful when you are training a dog with strong herding instincts, such as a Border Collie. It is much safer to keep them on a leash rather than risk them running into the road and trying to round up the traffic.

Accidents can happen

If the worst happens and your dog runs into the road and is hit by a car, it is important that it is taken to a vet as quickly as possible. Even if a dog seems unscathed or uninjured there may be internal damage that could cause problems if left undetected, so go for a checkup to ensure all is well. It is a good idea to program the telephone number of your vet into your cell phone, so that you always have the number available in an emergency situation. By telephoning ahead, you will enable staff at the office to prepare for your arrival. To keep a frightened, injured dog from biting or wriggling out of your arms as you remove it from the road, wrap it in a thick towel or a convenient item of clothing.

3 The next step is to take the dog to a busier road. When a car or truck goes past, the child should produce a favorite toy or treat to distract the dog. The dog should be rewarded with a toy or treat by obeying a simple command, such as "sit" or "down".

Tip to parents
Buy a high-visibility collar and leash for your child's dog so that drivers have a better chance of seeing it when you are walking together.

Problems with
puppy
passengers

"Are we nearly there yet?" There's a heartfelt plea that any parent will recognize. And, as any parent knows, a little forward planning can make the difference between a nightmare trip and a peaceful journey. When you are out traveling with your dog, whether it is on a short trip or a longer journey, you will need to plan and prepare just as meticulously.

Getting used to cars

Traveling in a car should be a vital part of the dog's socialization program and will help make sure that it doesn't become distressed by travel. As with children, never leave a dog unattended in your car because it can quickly become so hot that the dog can die.

You don't have to travel anywhere to get your dog used to being in the car. Simply sitting in a stationary car, while your child feeds the dog the odd treat and pets it quietly, will help. Once your dog is calm, you can take it on short drives, getting it out to do something enjoyable, such as a walk or a game in the park, before driving home again. If the only time the dog goes in the car is to do something stressful, such as visiting the vet, it will view traveling as a negative experience.

Some dogs are so eager to get into the car that they try to leap in before everyone else. This can be a nuisance, particularly if the dog is wet and muddy. From the beginning, put the dog into a sit and wait until you give permission to get in (see pages 80–81 for the "sit" command).

Car safety

Children are much less vulnerable to injury when they are traveling if they wear a seatbelt, and it is also possible to buy special harnesses for dogs. If you have to do an emergency stop it can be extremely dangerous to have a dog hurtling from the back seat into the front, so a harness or dog guard is an excellent investment. A small dog can be transported in puppy crate.

Going on vacation

Some boarding establishments view themselves as proper dog hotels, offering services such as

swimming pools, heated towel rails and haute cuisine! However, a regular boarding kennel is fine, as long as it is clean and the facilities are good. Personal recommendation from a friend or vet is a good starting point. Before booking in your dog, you should check that the place is hygienic and the dogs well cared for. Find out if the dogs are exercised every day or are simply given access to a run. You should avoid anywhere that does not insist on up-to-date vaccination certificates before accepting a dog.

ABOVE: The dog should be trained to always go into a sit before entering the car.

OPPOSITE: Sitting quietly in the stationary car with your child will help your dog get used to being inside a vehicle.

Once you are happy, you can arrange for your dog to get to know the place during a one-day, two-day or overnight visit, so that the longer stay does not come as such a shock. Pack its own bed, toys and a sweater or blanket that smells of home so the dog has a "security blanket" at night. Reassure your child that the dog will be kept warm and dry and fed and exercised regularly. You can explain that the dog will enjoy being in new surroundings with other dogs, and that you are sure it will be looked after safely.

Child's-eye view
"My dog loves being in the car. He sticks his head out of the window and his ears flap back, it's really funny." Paul, age 8

Tip to parents
If you allow your dog to travel in the car with its head out of the window, its eyes and ears are vulnerable to dust and debris. If is safer to put your dog in a harness so that it is not at risk.

How to be a
yard explorer

A dog enjoys exploring the outside world and your children will want to show it all their secret dens and hiding places. However, small puppies are agile and capable of getting through tiny gaps. If the yard hasn't been properly dog-proofed it could escape, putting it at risk of disease from contact with other animals (if it is unvaccinated) or injury from traffic.

Making the yard safe

Before you allow the dog into the yard, ask your children to go around every square inch of it, looking for small places that a puppy can hide or little gaps in the fence that it may be able to wriggle through.

Ask children to make a "please close the gate" note, which you can laminate and position at child's-eye level to help remind them and their friends.

Ask children to tidy away small toys or objects a dog might chew.

Mend any holes or loose panels in fences. Check hedges and block up any gaps.

Attach chicken wire or mesh to the bottom of metal gates that a small puppy could squeeze through.

Consider rehanging the gates so that they open inward, making it more difficult for a dog to push its way out.

Put locks on sheds and garages to keep out a curious dog.

Put all chemicals, such as weedkiller, paints and antifreeze, on a high shelf; dogs are attracted to a chemical used in slug pellets, so be particularly careful with this product. Keep garage floors clean so that a puppy doesn't step in anything chemical and ingest it later when licking itself.

Poisonous plants

Some plants can be poisonous to puppies. A full list of these can be found on the Internet. However, if your dog is entertained by your children and having fun, it is unlikely it will be bored enough to start eating plants.

Run for it

Some people find it convenient to have an outdoor run and kennel area where they can put the dog occasionally when they have to go out. As long as this a secure area, with a kennel containing a comty bed, toys to play with and fresh water to drink, this can be a good solution. Dogs should not be left unattended for longer than four hours, however, or they can become bored and develop negative habits, such as prolonged barking, digging or chewing.

First steps outside

Your children may be desperate to have the dog accompany them to school, but first it will have to complete its vaccinations. This usually happens at about 12 weeks. However, you should encourage the puppy to go into the yard to relieve itself as soon as possible, so that it realizes this is the place to go. A small dog could always be carried to school occasionally, to experience the sights and smells along the way and to get used to being the center of attention.

ABOVE: Boisterious games in the yard are a great way of using up surplus canine energy, and ensuring your child gets lots of exercise, too!

LEFT: Your child can help ensure that there is fresh water available for your dog when it is in the garden, whatever the time of year.

OPPOSITE: Keep dogs away from gardening equipment and other potential dangers. Anything that might harm the puppy should be put away in a shed or other secure storage area.

Puppy safety
all year round

As your child's puppy grows, you will find that each season brings its own special joys. However, it's also useful to consider in advance the pitfalls that you might need to watch out for at different times of year. With determination and good planning, you will be able to avoid costly vet's bills and make sure that the dog enjoys year-round fun with the whole family.

Summer hazards

Make sure that your children are aware of the dangers that hot weather can pose for their dog. They might be enjoying themselves so much that they forget that the dog might not be having as much fun. Heat can be the worst problem. Dogs cannot perspire and quickly become overheated. Symptoms such as excessive panting, drooling and restlessness might require urgent veterinary attention. You should also ask your children to be vigilant that their dog doesn't get accidentally locked into a hot spot, such as a greenhouse. If the dog goes into the yard, there should be shaded areas to which it can retreat. Take it indoors to a cool room during the hottest part of the day. Extra grooming or a haircut can make your dog more comfortable in summer.

At any time of year, you should take plenty of fresh drinking water with you on long walks or if you are transporting your dog to the beach. Children can be responsible for carrying the traveling water bottle and offering water to the dog. They should stop the dog from drinking from stagnant ponds or puddles, which may contain toxic blue-green algae.

If your dog swims in the ocean make sure you always wash him off afterward, because dried sand and saltwater can irritate the skin. Make a note of tide times, and take care that the dog doesn't become exhausted. Boisterous games should be kept shorter than usual, because very young and older dogs don't always have the sense to stop when they are tired. The whole family will also need to supervise dogs carefully during picnics and barbecues, to make sure they don't eat something indigestible, such as a husk of corn or shish-kebab stick.

Child's-eye view
"I want to build snowmen with my dog. We could make a snow dog too." Annie, age 5

Tip to parents
Children and dogs playing in the snow are a joy to see, but limit the time they spend doing this. Snow sticks to a dog's coat and can ball up in its feet, so dry it off thoroughly when it comes indoors. Exposure to subzero temperatures can cause frostbite of the nose, ears and feet. If your dog's paws look red, gray or are peeling, wrap the dog in warm towels and seek veterinary advice.

Question time

Q *What should we do to help if an insect stings our dog?*

Bee and wasp stings usually occur on the dog's nose, mouth or paws. Some animals may have an allergic reaction, and if your dog suffers excessive swelling or difficulty breathing seek urgent attention. Bee stings are acidic. If the sting is visible remove it with tweezers and bathe the area with a baking soda solution. Wasp stings are alkaline, and the sting is not left in the skin. Bathing with a weak solution of vinegar will soothe the affected area. If you suspect a snake has bitten your dog, contact your vet immediately.

A If you think an insect has stung the dog, try to find an adult to help. If you have seen what kind of insect it is, it will make the treatment easier. If we can see the sting we'll need to take it out carefully with tweezers and bathe the area to soothe it. Wasps don't leave their stings behind, but we can bathe the area to make it feel better. If the dog doesn't recover quickly or cannot breathe easily it may be having an allergic reaction, so we should take it to the vet.

Winter blues

Your children will be wrapped up with scarves and gloves when they take their dog for a walk, but don't let them think that the dog's fur coat will be sufficient to keep it warm in the coldest weather. Wind chill can cause temperatures to drop sharply. Dogs with thin coats and older dogs with reduced body mass will need a coat in winter to keep them warm. Make sure that outdoor kennels are raised off the ground and are warm and free from drafts, but bring dogs inside as much as possible. Older dogs will appreciate an extra fleecy blanket on their beds.

After a walk, ask your children to wash the dog's paws in lukewarm water to remove ice, salt or grit. (If you keep the hair between your dog's toes trimmed, you will find it easier to spot anything hidden there.) You can also ask your children to check every day that the dog's outdoor water bowls do not ice over.

If your dog falls into an icy lake or river, get it out as fast as possible. It may be suffering from hypothermia, so wrap it in a warm blanket and seek veterinary advice.

Protect dogs and children from dangerous winter items. Put fireguards in place around fires and portable heaters, and make sure that heaters are out of reach. Store antifreeze and windshield wiper fluids safely; many are toxic but taste sweet, and your dog may be attracted to them.

chapter 8
What if?

Each phase of your dog's life will bring its pleasures and problems. This chapter examines some of the challenges and explores how children can help you deal with them. Even trained dogs can develop behavioral problems, such as excessive barking or fussy eating, or they might suffer from psychological difficulties, such as anxiety. The child-dog relationship can also become problematic at different times in the child's or dog's life. Given patience, these problems can be resolved.

Old age
As your dog enters its senior years it will need more care and attention. Thankfully, nutrition and veterinary medicine has advanced so much that dogs are living longer and now have an average age of about 12 years. Smaller dogs tend to live longer than the larger breeds, often carrying on happily into their late teens.

Nevertheless, as dogs grow older, they gradually slow down, particularly if they develop joint problems, such as arthritis. If your dog seems to be grumpier than usual when your children play with it, it may be reacting to pain. Your vet may be able to recommend special treatments and also give you some pain management tips that will help your dog enjoy life to the fullest for longer.

Dinner time
Pet-food manufacturers have developed a range of dog foods designed to fulfill the changing nutritional needs of older dogs. Older dogs tend to move around less and can therefore be prone to obesity, which increases the pressure on their joints. Make children aware that too many treats or human food snacks are not good for the dog.

Some veterinary offices run geriatric clinics for dogs, where blood pressure, weight and other vital signs are measured and you can get expert nutritional advice.

Exercise
An older dog can sometimes seem reluctant to go out, particularly in bad weather, but encouraging your children to take it out for regular, gentle exercise for short periods will help lubricate its joints and improve its mobility. Drying the dog off gently with a warm towel if it comes back wet will be appreciated, as will an extra blanket and a coat.

Explain to the children that their dog will not be able to play for as long or run as quickly as it grows older. Point out that it can be fun to think up games that have a slower pace, such as laying treasure trails of treats around the house, so that the dog can move from room to room looking for them rather than spending too long lying on its bed.

Putting your dog's bed somewhere in the middle of the home, such as the family room, will help it feel a part of family life even though it can't follow everyone around like it used to do. Ramps to get up and down to favorite spots will also help make life easier.

When you need
a little
help

If your dog has previously been well behaved but suddenly develops behavioral problems, such as barking, biting, chewing or exhibiting signs of anxiety, it is important to find out the underlying cause of the new behavior. Once this has been identified, the whole family should work together to help the dog overcome the problems.

Ask the vet

Many physical problems can cause changes in behavior, so before you do anything else take the dog to your vet for a checkup to get a clean bill of health. If the behavioral problems are very severe and badly affecting family life, your vet may recommend that the dog is referred to a professional animal behavior counselor for specific advice.

My dog's a bully!

If your dog starts guarding its food whenever anyone walks past or growls when you want to take a toy from it, it's time to take action. Don't wait until the behavior becomes deeply engrained or it will be much more difficult to change. Allowing your dog to rule the roost is a recipe for disaster. Make sure that your dog understands that it is not the leader of the family pack and that it knows its place in the family's pecking order (see pages 68–69).

Help! He won't get off my leg!

Mounting behavior can be another sign of the dog trying to assert its dominance. You can deal with this embarrassing problem by following a behavior modification program that reinforces the dog's subordinate position in the family pack. Neutering may also be an answer (see page 69).

LEFT: Food guarding should be dealt with as early as possible, before behavior such as snapping develops.

OPPOSITE: To kick the barking habit, praise your puppy when it is quiet and ignore it whenever it becomes very vocal.

Question time

Q *Why does the dog keep running off with my toys? He's got loads of his own.*
If your children run after the dog and chase it whenever it grabs one of their toys it will probably think it's a great game. Equally, if they grab it off the dog and wave it in the air they will simply signal that they are keen for the game to continue. Try to explain that keeping calm and walking past the dog, dropping a food treat nearby as a distraction or offering one of the dog's own favorite toys, will be a more effective way of getting it to leave their toys alone. Once it realizes that the only time it gets a game is when it plays with its own toys, it should start to leave your children's toys alone.

A He may think it's a game, especially if you run after him and try to grab it off him. Keep calm and use a food treat or one of the dog's special toys to distract him. He needs to realize that he only gets to play with you if he is playing with his own toys.

Stop barking!

Dogs that bark incessantly can be real nuisances, for yourselves and for your neighbors. Behaviorists believe that attention-seeking behavior, such as constant barking, tail chasing, paw chewing or licking, is best ignored as much as possible. As with children, rewarding attention-seeking behavior with attention, even if it is very negative attention, will only help reinforce the behavior you don't want.

The trick with barking is to reward the dog with praise and attention when it is quiet and calm and to walk away or put the dog in another room when it is not. If a particular situation triggers the barking, such as the doorbell ringing, you can enlist the help of your children to embark on a training program. Ask the children to ring the doorbell and immediately tell the dog to go to its bed and offer a treat, such as food or a favorite toy. Practice this a lot so that the dog begins to associate the doorbell ringing with going to its bed and getting a treat.

Flushing out housebreaking problems

Dogs are usually easy to housebreak, particularly if your child has had it from a puppy and has consistently taken it outside when it wakes up or has finished eating. However, problems can still arise. Puppy training pads are a temporary indoor solution, but don't rely on them for too long or you will have difficulty in persuading your puppy to go outside.

Training regimes

Remind your child that puppies have smaller bladders than larger dogs and find it more difficult to retain urine, so they will need to go outside more often. Don't withhold water from the dog at night to try to housebreak it: water is vital for hydration and optimum health.

Your child should stay calm and patient when housebreaking a dog. Shouting or physical punishment will make the dog anxious and exacerbate the problem so the process takes even longer. Behaviorists have observed that fear and excitement are two of the main causes of incontinence, although an older dog may simply have trouble getting to the door in time. If this is the case, you may have to wake it up and take it outside before it leaves it too long. Dogs that have been in a shelter for a long time may need to be completely retrained, although some get the hang of things very quickly.

In recent years, some manufacturers have developed pheromone-enriched markers to train dogs to urinate in a specific place outdoors. This pheromone is a synthetic version of a natural substance produced by dogs. The post is simply pushed into a grassy area of the garden to encourage dogs to go there.

Clean up

Older children can help you to clean any areas where your dog has an accident, mopping thoroughly with a suitable stain- and odor-removing product. Explain that this will get rid of the smell and help deter the dog from going there again. It might be a good idea to remove the puppy calmly from the room before cleaning up, as your body language might communicate

Tip to parents

Make sure that someone accompanies the puppy every time it goes outside so that you can be certain it does relieve itself and can be praised immediately.

Question time

Q *Why is our puppy dry in the day but not at night?*

It may be some weeks before your puppy can go all night without emptying its bladder. Newspaper or a puppy training pad near the door help minimize mess. If you put a puppy in an indoor crate at night, it will be reluctant to soil its own sleeping area, although this will not help it learn to go to the door.

A It's just because he's little and can't go all through the night yet. You were the same when you were very small. We need to take him out as much as possible and put some newspapers on the floor by the door or in his crate so that he learns that this is the correct place to go.

annoyance and frighten the puppy, making it more likely to be nervous and make similar mistakes in the future.

Watch it!

As with other behavior problems, take your dog to the vet for a checkup if housebreaking problems develop suddenly. Once the vet assures everything is okay, you can investigate possible causes and try to rectify the situation. A change in

the dog's routine may have caused a setback in training. Tell your children that feeding at the same time each day and going outside within 20 minutes of eating is very important, because this is usually when a puppy needs to empty its bowels. When a puppy first arrives, it should be taken outside every couple of hours.

Everyone should learn the signs that your dog needs to relieve itself. It may start sniffing, circling or even go to the door and scratch at it, and this is when your child can take it outside and give a verbal command, such as "toilet". She should try to get the puppy to walk outside rather than carrying it out, because this will help it learn to go to the door and ask to go out. She should give her dog lots of praise every time it goes in the right place.

ABOVE: Encourage your child to get in the habit of taking the dog outside when it wakes up and after every meal.

LEFT: Any traces of an accident indoors should be thoroughly mopped up, so the smell doesn't encourage the puppy to repeat the performance.

OPPOSITE: Scratching at the door is a sign that your puppy wants to go outside to relieve itself.

Fussy eaters
and greedy guts

As parents we love to see our children enjoying the right sort of healthy food and leaving empty plates. When this happens the effort involved in preparing nutritious meals seems worthwhile. However, children are certainly not always interested in eating the food that we think is good for them, and dogs can sometimes be just as fickle.

Fusspots

Some owners have reported that their dogs refuse to eat the food in their bowl unless they are spoon-fed. Unfortunately, as with young children, rewarding fussy eaters with extra attention or a range of several choices and flavors, simply makes the situation worse.

If your dog is a fussy eater, first take it to the vet for a physical checkup to rule out a medical cause for the behavior. Once all is confirmed to be okay it is probably time for you to adopt a tough-love approach to its diet.

Choose a complete dog food (which provides all the nutrition that your dog needs) and put its daily portion down in a clean dish at meal times. Explain to your children why they shouldn't try to hand-feed the dog or pay extra attention to it if it turns up his nose at what they are offering. After 20 minutes, if the food hasn't been eaten, simply remove and dispose of it. Wet food deteriorates very quickly, particularly in hot weather, and bacteria may affect its palatability, so don't be tempted to keep it until the next day.

Most dog behaviorists predict that repeating this exercise over a few days will soon produce an improvement in your dog's eating habits. Make sure that your children are not sneaking the dog treats or things from their own plates because they feel sorry for it or because they want to offload things they don't like eating themselves.

LEFT: Energetic games in the park are a fun way of keeping dogs and children healthy.

OPPOSITE: A greedy dog may even knock over the kitchen garbage can to see what tasty treats are lurking inside. Dispose of leftover food securely so that the dog isn't tempted to forage.

Too fat

If you take your dog for an annual checkup, your vet will weigh it and tell you if it is putting on too much weight. Obesity is just as dangerous for dogs as it is for children and adults, so step up its exercise program, reduce calorie intake and encourage your children to play with it more so that it regains its fitness. One of the best things about owning a dog is that it can help everyone in the family keep fit.

On the scrounge

Dogs are natural scavengers and they may knock over trash cans, or even work the foot pedal, in order to get at the contents, even if they are fed sufficient food by their owners. They may ingest things that are potentially dangerous to them, such as bones or plastic packaging. If this is a problem, get a strong can with a lid that is difficult to open, or reposition the can in a locked cupboard or utility room.

Child's-eye view

"I sometimes daydream when I'm eating, especially if I'm watching the television, and then our dog sneaks up and eat things off my plate. It makes me mad but I still love him."
Andrew, age 9

Tip to parents

Some dogs are tempted by the smell of food, and if your dog is a bit of a thief it may be easiest to shut it out of the room when the children are eating. Discourage your children from wandering around while they eat because the sight of a chocolate bar or cookie being paraded at eye level might prove irresistible!

Encouraging
bravery

There are many examples of how courageous dogs can be. Even small dogs can be brave when it comes to protecting their owners and homes from intruders. However, it's important that your children recognize that all dogs are different and that their tolerance levels to things such as noise will vary – some appear oblivious, whereas others are terrified.

Fright night

Sometimes fear can affect dogs so much that they will run off in a panic and are unable to find their way home again, which can be distressing for everyone. Fireworks are used in celebrations at various times throughout the year, and thunder and lightning storms can make some dogs tremble with nerves.

You may be able to pinpoint your dog's initial bad experience, perhaps when it was a puppy, or it may be something that you will never understand. Whatever the reason for the fear, a desensitization program is far more effective than rewarding negative reactions with extra cuddling and praise.

Q *How do we find our dog?*
If your dog goes missing, get your children to make posters with an up-to-date photograph of the dog. Distribute them in your neighborhood. Put fliers in your neighbors' mailboxes asking them to check sheds and garages. An ad in your local paper or on the radio may also yield results. Report the dog missing to the company that holds your dog's microchip database and inform your vet, local animal shelters, police and the pound. Search areas repeatedly at different times of the day, and if necessary offer a reward.

A There's a lot we can do. You can help by making posters and pinning them to trees and signposts. We need to let as many people as possible know that he's missing, so tell all your friends and ask them to help look for him too. We'll stand a much better chance of getting him home safely if we search different areas at different times. We'll also put an advert in the paper, and we mustn't forget to tell his microchip company and the vet.

ABOVE: Your child can help accustom your dog to threatening noises recorded on a CD. This should be played quietly while the dog is doing something fun, to create new associations in the dog's mind.

OPPOSITE: Hiding under or behind furniture is a classic fear response in dogs. Don't fuss over the animal when it does this, or you will reinforce the insecurities.

If your dog always runs and hides behind the sofa every time it hears a loud noise it can be tempting to pull the dog out and comfort it, but this simply reinforces his behavior. Ask everyone to ignore the dog and behave as normally as possible, so that it does not pick up messages that it is right to be worried. Try to send out relaxed signals, such as yawning, lying down or slow blinking, and don't stare at the dog even if it is looking to you for reassurance. It will pick up on your body language, so make sure the message is, "It's all okay, there's nothing to worry about."

If your dog shows extreme fear your vet may suggest testing its hearing to make sure it has no hypersensitivity to noise. A low dose of tranquilizers may provide a short-term solution, but desensitization is the best long-term plan.

Desensitize

You can buy a plug-in dog-appeasing pheromone (DAP) dispenser, which some dogs find calming,

although it is useful only if you can predict when a storm or firework display is due to start. The pheromones are synthetic versions of natural substances produced by lactating bitches three to five days after birth, to relax and reassure the pups, so by plugging in a DAP you will remind your puppy subconsciously of its mom. Your vet may be able to supply or source these for you.

Listen up

Specialists in animal behavior have developed CDs that have been designed to accustom pets gradually to the particular sound that frightens them, whether it is fireworks or thunder. Your child can simply play the CD at the lowest level when the dog is doing something pleasurable, such as eating, playing a game or being stroked. Gradually, over the next few days and weeks, ask your child to increase the volume until the dog tolerates the noise without fearful reactions, such as panting, trembling, licking his lips or hiding.

Mediating
child-dog
relations

The relationship between a child and her dog is not always smooth. Problems range from pestering the animal to being jealous of the attention it receives, or ignoring it completely as the child grows older. If problems are left for too long they become difficult to resolve, so act quickly. Your vet may have useful advice or be able to recommend an experienced behaviorist or counselor.

My teenage son ignores the dog

When children grow into young adults they may consider demonstrations of affection toward the family pet as "uncool", childish behavior. However, if anything were to happen to the dog they would no doubt be just as upset as anyone else. If your child has responsibilities for the dog's care, such as walking or feeding, these should continue or it will affect the dog's well-being. Otherwise, provided your dog gets attention from other family members, it should not be too affected by this passing phase in your teenager's life.

The youth section of your national kennel club will have many teenage members who are involved in fun and exciting activities. Find out if there is anything planned for your area that might interest your teenager.

My daughter pesters the dog

Some dogs are tolerant of childish attention, but others are less so. Older dogs can develop joint problems and may express pain in a grumpy, growling way. Explain that your dog doesn't appreciate being handled all the time, especially if she is carrying it everywhere, as it makes it feel insecure. Agree on when play times will be and how long they will last and encourage her to involve the dog in interactive games, such as fetching a ball, so that they engage with each other positively. Afterward, try to find fun activities to distract your daughter from the dog.

Our kids have lost interest now the puppy is fully grown

Think of some activities they can do together, such as throwing a party for their friends and dogs (see pages 94–95). Vary walk routes so they

aren't boring and ask your children where they'd like to go. Explain that the dog is a family member, not a toy that can be abandoned, and encourage them to become responsible owners.

My child is jealous of our puppy

Pets and children need time to get used to each other, so supervise them carefully. Encourage your child to play with the dog. Give your child lots of attention, positively reinforcing her behavior with praise, so that it is an enjoyable experience. Ignore unwanted behavior, such as sulking, as much as possible, using distraction techniques to divert her attention in a positive way.

My son's friend is scared of dogs

You probably need to contact the boy's parents and find out their attitude toward dogs. If they are communicating their own fears it will be harder for your child's friend to overcome his anxiety. Some children are afraid that the dog will knock them over or bite them, and it may be that in time this boy will feel reassured that your dog is well behaved and harmless.

My nephew is allergic to dogs

Despite your best efforts, your nephew may experience some allergic reaction, so make sure that he has enough medication for any visits, particularly sleepovers. If he is coming for a short visit try to keep the dog in an outdoor kennel, and vacuum the house thoroughly at least two hours beforehand. Vacuuming just before a visit is worse than doing nothing at all because it takes two hours for the dust to settle, and the dust could trigger an attack as much as the dog hair. Don't forget to vacuum all the curtains and loose covers, which are dust traps and often forgotten. Damp-dusting with a weak solution of water and vinegar will help rid your house of dust.

What if a dog chases your child?

Teach your child to "act like a tree" — that is, stand very still and quietly. Running away will simply encourage the dog to chase after her. If she is sitting down or is knocked down by a dog, the child should "act like a rock", curling up on one side with her fists over her ears. If she is afraid the dog is going to bite, encourage her to throw something as bait, such as a backpack or jacket.

If your child is on a bicycle, the spinning of a bike's wheels and pedals may excite the dog. Encourage your child to stop her bike and dismount, saying "no" loudly. If she has a water bottle, a spray of this toward the dog may help distract it.

ABOVE: If you have more than one child, you may find that one sibling becomes jealous of a new puppy and its bond with the other sibling. Make sure you give everyone in the family lots of attention.

OPPOSITE: When children become teenagers, they may lose interest in the dog. Give the dog lots of extra love and allow the teenager space while the phase passes.

Saying goodbye
and hello

Ideally, your dog will enjoy a long and happy life with your family, and it is everyone's dream that a beloved older dog will simply die in its sleep, so that nobody has to make a decision about euthanasia. However, accidents and illness or deterioration in the dog's quality of life sometimes mean that euthanasia is the most humane step for you to take.

ABOVE: Drawing pictures of their pet and writing about it can help children come to terms with their grief at its death.

OPPOSITE: As an animal ages or becomes ill, your child may be distressed that it can no longer play with her in the old way. Explain that it is at a stage in its life when it needs special care from its family.

Grief

The loss of a family pet is often a child's first experience of death and grieving, and how much you explain about what has happened will depend on the child's age and level of emotional maturity. A child may be much more stalwart and accepting than many adults and often copes better as a result. If your dog is very old, you can try to prepare children for the inevitable, so that it does not come as a complete shock. It's best to avoid the phrase "the dog was put to sleep", as this can make young children anxious about going to sleep themselves.

Psychologists recognize that there are several distinct phases to the grieving process for both adults and children:

Anticipated loss This occurs particularly with a very old dog or one that has had a prolonged illness.
Shock and denial These reactions are common immediately after death, particularly if a healthy dog has been involved in an accident.
Emotional suffering The familiar middle phase, when crying and talking about the dog can seem very painful.
Recovery This stage occurs when, finally, your child can accept the situation and it is possible to move on.

If your child seems stuck in any stage of the grieving process your vet may be able to offer a bereavement counseling service. Alternatively, your doctor may recommend a specialized counselor. Encouraging children to write and talk about the dog, draw pictures or make a photo album will all be helpful. Tell your child's teacher if you have lost a family pet.

When is it time?

Talk to the vet about your dog's quality of life and if there is anything more he can to do to help. Generally, if a dog is in constant pain, is unable to move, cannot eat or drink properly or is totally incapacitated it may be kindest to let the vet intervene. Euthanasia is a painless procedure, involving an injection to put the dog to sleep and then a second one to stop the heart. It takes seconds, and vets are very experienced at dealing with it. Most encourage owners to be present if they wish. Beforehand, consider whether you want to take the dog home to bury in the yard or if you want a cremation.

Question time

Q *Can I have another dog?*
When everyone in the family accepts the loss of the dog and can talk about it without sadness you might be able to welcome another one into your life. However, no dog will ever replace one that you have owned for years, and you might like to get another breed or type of dog to avoid comparisons. If your circumstances have changed, consider if you can offer another dog a loving home for life. See the first chapter of this book for advice on what your dog will need.

A We need to be sure that everyone in the family is not still so sad that they don't give a new dog all the love it deserves. And we need to think about what kind of dog we'd like, because we'll never get another one like Toby, and it wouldn't be fair to expect a new dog to be just like him. Perhaps choosing another breed altogether will make it easier. Let's think about the kind of dog can we give a home to.

Index

Page numbers in *italics* refer to illustrations.

Acknowledgments

Author acknowledgments

Many thanks to the primary school children —and their teachers—of Gonerby Hill Foot School, Grantham, for allowing me to chat to them and get a child's-eye view of what they think about dogs.

Thanks also to my lovely daughter, Madeline Joy Lainchbury, and her friends for their patience as I constantly picked their brains about what they thought was involved in looking after a dog. Their responses helped me uncover those areas of care that parents need most help in explaining.

I was invited to spend a day at a Young Kennel Club summer camp, where I was able to talk to trainers, parents and kids and was amazed at how knowledgeable and enthusiastic everyone was. It was inspirational to see so many children, teenagers and dogs enjoying themselves together and taking part in different activities.

Finally, thanks to my good friend Rick and his dog Oscar, who taught me a lot and made me smile in the process.

I'm grateful to you all for your help and advice in writing this book.

Photographic acknowledgments

Special Photography: © Octopus Publishing Group Limited/Russell Sadur.

Other photography: © Octopus Publishing Group Limited/Janeanne Gilchrist 96; /Steve Gorton 44–5; /Angus Murray/Steve Gorton 77 right.

Publisher acknowledgments

The publisher would like to thank all the children who were photographed for this book (and their parents and guardians for bringing them along): Alice Golding, Amelia Badenoch, Annie Weller, Cameron Thomson, Charlotte Ford, Charlotte Lee, Daniel Baxter, Ella Roscoe, Finlay Thomson, Fleur Bruneau-Cordell, Gabriella Turk, Greg Williams, James Golding, Jemma Austin, Kira Taylor, Leonardo Martini, Madeline Lainchbury, Nina Roscoe, Olivia Morrison, Phoebe Morrison, Polly Hardwicke, Rebecca Lawler, Sol Headley, Sophia Turk, Thomas Bruneau-Cordell, William Mason, Zara Williams. Thanks also to Sandra Strong and Jeanette Miller of Dogs on Camera.

Executive editor: Trevor Davies
Editor: Fiona Robertson
Executive art editors: Mark Stevens and
    Karen Sawyer
Designer: Mark Stevens
Photographer: Russell Sadur
Senior production controller: Martin Croshaw